The Prayer of Illumination

The Prayer of Illumination

A Comparative Analysis into the Eastern and Reformed Nature of the Mar Thoma Syrian Church

ABRAHAM KURUVILLA

WIPF & STOCK · Eugene, Oregon

THE PRAYER OF ILLUMINATION
A Comparative Analysis into the Eastern and Reformed Nature
of the Mar Thoma Syrian Church

Copyright © 2022 Abraham Kuruvilla. All rights reserved. Except for brief quotations in critical publications or reviews, no part of this book may be reproduced in any manner without prior written permission from the publisher. Write: Permissions, Wipf and Stock Publishers, 199 W. 8th Ave., Suite 3, Eugene, OR 97401.

Wipf & Stock
An Imprint of Wipf and Stock Publishers
199 W. 8th Ave., Suite 3
Eugene, OR 97401

www.wipfandstock.com

PAPERBACK ISBN: 978-1-6667-0664-2
HARDCOVER ISBN: 978-1-6667-0665-9
EBOOK ISBN: 978-1-6667-0666-6

JANUARY 12, 2022 11:05 AM

Dedicated to my wife, Ann, and baby, Andrew

Contents

List of Tables | viii

Acknowledgments | ix

Abbreviations | x

Introduction | xi

CHAPTER 1
  A Brief Introduction of the Mar Thoma Syrian Church | 1

CHAPTER 2
  The Prayer for Illumination: Address and Petition | 4

CHAPTER 3
  The Prayer for Illumination: Fruit and Doxology | 40

CHAPTER 4
  Conclusion | 50

Bibliography | 63

List of Tables

Comparison of Prayer for Illumination | 7

Acknowledgments

I WOULD LIKE TO acknowledge my teachers, church community, and my fellow priest. The faith and practices of the Mar Thoma Syrian Church have played an important role in the formation of this book. I would like to extend a special word of thanks for the late lamented His Grace Rt. Rev. Dr. Joseph Mar Thoma Metropolitan and Rt. Rev. Dr. Isaac Mar Philoxenos. Their guidance and support were pivotal in my higher studies. I would also like to acknowledge Dr. Bruce McCormack and Dr. James Kay for their guidance and support during my study at Princeton Theological Seminary.

Abbreviations

MTC: Mar Thoma Church
MTL: Mar Thoma Liturgy

Introduction

THE BOOK LOOKS INTO the liturgy of the Mar Thoma Church. The Mar Thoma Church claims to be eastern and reformed. An enquiry is made into the liturgy of the Eucharist to look into the prayer for illumination. The measuring rod to determine the eastern and the reformed nature is the eastern fathers such as Gregory Nazianzen, Athanasius, St. Basil, etc., and the reformer John Calvin. The prayer for illumination, as laid out in the eucharistic liturgy of the Mar Thoma Church, is compared to the prayer for illumination in the Syrian liturgy and the Genevan Psalter. Some observations are made and accordingly conclusions are drawn. Based on the conclusions, some implications are made for the Mar Thoma Church.

CHAPTER 1

A Brief Introduction of the Mar Thoma Syrian Church[1]

A PROPER STARTING POINT for an introduction to the Mar Thoma Syrian Church would be perhaps explaining the title itself. The title "Mar Thoma" means St. Thomas. As the title suggests, there is a connection with St. Thomas, the apostle of Jesus Christ. It is believed that the Mar Thoma Syrian Church[2] was founded by St. Thomas, the apostle of Jesus Christ. This claim has been well researched in terms of its historicity.[3]

The mention of "Syrian" in the title suggests that there is some connection to the East of the world. This connection to the East was a result of a migration that happened from the East to the south of India.[4] Until now, we have been trying to understand

---

1. The introduction and chapter 1 were previously published in my book *Eastern and Reformed*, published by Wipf and Stock in 2018. The first chapter is included in this book because an introduction to the history and the nature of the Mar Thoma Syrian Church is needed before doing a doctrinal analysis.

2. From now on I will refer to the Mar Thoma Syrian Church as the Mar Thoma Church and abbreviate it as MTC.

3. Missick, "Mar Thoma," 52–59. For a brief reading into the historicity see John, "Liturgy of the Mar Thoma Syrian Church," 1–3.

4. Missick, "Mar Thoma," 45–50.

The Prayer of Illumination

the MTC on the basis of the title. However, to conclude an understanding of the MTC only on the basis of the title would lead to an incomplete understanding of the MTC. So it is necessary to mention that the unique characteristic of the MTC is that it is reformed.[5] This reformed characteristic was a result of the reformation that happened in the Mar Thoma Church some two hundred years ago.[6] So, we can say that the MTC is arguably founded by St. Thomas, it has a connection to the East of the world, which gives the MTC an eastern nature, and it is reformed.

We can safely conclude that the MTC has a mixed history, which is a combination of eastern elements and reformed principles. However, irrespective of the above two claims, there is a lot of ambiguity regarding the theological nature of the MTC. There are sections in the MTC that arguably claim that the MTC is eastern. However, there also exists another section in the MTC that arguably claims that the MTC is reformed. Though the historicity of such claims are well-researched and credible, in terms of doctrine and theological nature such claims are arguable because they are not credibly founded. There definitely exist some eastern elements and also reformed elements in the MTC. However, to claim that the MTC is *only eastern* in its theological nature or *only reformed* in its theological nature is always debatable. Such arguable and debatable claims linger on in sections of the clergy, the faithful, and also in the general understanding of the MTC by the outside world at large. As a result, there is always a trend of overemphasizing the importance of either the eastern elements over the reformed elements or vice-versa.

A logical and credible starting point from this reality of arguable and overemphasized ambiguity would be to map the eastern and reformed elements in the MTC. The process of mapping would involve pointing out the respective elements as and where it is evident. This process of mapping would necessarily involve a comparison with the eastern and reformed doctrines or beliefs

---

5. John, "Liturgy of the Mar Thoma Syrian Church," 4–7.

6. For a detailed reading into formation of the Mar Thoma Syrian Church see Varughese, "Religion, Renaissance and Protest," 170–80.

A Brief Introduction of the Mar Thoma Syrian Church

as found in the global church. Toward this endeavor I will make an effort of equating the beliefs of the MTC with the eastern and reformed doctrines or beliefs as found in the global church. Along with this, there will be a systematic analysis of the beliefs. Such a combination of mapping, equating, and analyzing would make the claims of the MTC credible. However, since the effort of this book is an enquiry into the theological nature of the MTC, I will be spending a considerable amount of time with one or two elements at a time. Accordingly, this book is an effort toward mapping the eastern and reformed elements with regards to the doctrine of atonement and Holy Spirit as found in the MTC.

The question before us is: how do we start the process of mapping the theological nature of the MTC? In other words, what is the source to enquire for mapping the theological nature of the MTC? Unlike some churches, the MTC does not have a documented copy of its theology in detail. However, one of the characteristics of eastern churches is that its theology is found in its liturgy.[7] To begin a mapping process with the understanding that the theology of the MTC is found in the liturgy should not be misunderstood that we are concluding even before we start that the MTC is eastern. Using liturgy as a source of inquiry should only be a starting point. However, it should be understood that the Mar Thoma liturgy[8] is not an explicit confessional document regarding the doctrines of Christian faith pertaining to the MTC. Such an endeavor has never been attempted in the MTC, and hence this book is important as it will give clarity with regards to the theological and confessional standpoint of the MTC.

---

7. Patros Yousif connects the Syriac liturgy to Syriac spirituality. See Yousif, "East Syrian Spirituality," 112–33.

8. The liturgy of the Mar Thoma Church; hereafter referred to as MTL.

Chapter 2

The Prayer for Illumination
Address and Petition

THE HOLY SPIRIT PLAYS a vital role in the life of the church. The Holy Spirit assists us in our faith formation. The thesis of this book is that in the liturgy of the Mar Thoma Church (MTC) we find a combination of eastern and reformed views of the Holy Spirit. By eastern and reformed I mean the doctrine of the Holy Spirit as taught by the eastern fathers as well as reformers like John Calvin. Accordingly, the doctrine of Holy Spirit in the MTC will be evaluated against the teaching of eastern fathers and that of John Calvin. The MTC claims to be eastern and reformed. However, such a claim has to be theologically grounded. If my thesis is proven to be true then I will be able to theologically ground the eastern and reformed nature of the MTC.

Furthermore, though an explicit understanding of the nature and work of the Holy Spirit is found in the Mar Thoma Liturgy (MTL), I will limit this book to the illumination of the Holy Spirit as seen in the prayer for illumination. Throughout this book I will compare the prayer for illumination of the MTL alongside that of the Syrian Liturgy and the Genevan Psalter. In such comparison, I will simultaneously do a descriptive mapping and a theological

The Prayer for Illumination: Address and Petition

analysis of the eastern and reformed dimensions in the prayer for illumination in the MTL. Then a conclusion will be drawn whether the MTL agrees, disagrees, or mediates with the eastern and the reformed point of view. This effort will help me to go forward with a constructive work in the future. Such an endeavor has never been attempted in the MTC and hence this book is important for me as it will give clarity with regards to the theological standpoint of the MTC.[1]

I will first lay out the prayer for illumination of the Syrian Liturgy, the MTL, and the Genevan Psalter.

THE SYRIAN LITURGY

The prayer for illumination in the Syrian Liturgy is as follows:

> Grant us, o Lord God, the knowledge of Thy divine words, and fill us with the understanding of Thy holy Gospel, and the richness of Thy divine gifts and the grace of Thy Holy Spirit. Grant us that with joy we may keep Thy commandments and accomplish and fulfill Thy will, and be accounted worthy of the blessings and the mercies which are from Thee, now and at all times.[2]

THE MAR THOMA LITURGY

The prayer of illumination in the MTL is as follows:

> O Lord God, give to us knowledge and discernment of your divine words. Fill us with the truth of your holy Gospel, the riches of your holy wisdom and the gift of

---

1. The title "Mar Thoma" means St. Thomas. The Mar Thoma Church (MTC) has a mixed history, which is a combination of eastern elements (which the MTC arguably claims go back to St. Thomas coming to India) and reformed principles (which was a result of the reformation that happened in the MTC some two hundred years ago). For a detailed reading into formation of the Mar Thoma Syrian Church see Varughese, "Religion, Renaissance and Protest," 170–80.

2. *Anaphora*, 22.

The Prayer of Illumination

your Holy Spirit. Enable us gladly to obey your commands and perfectly to fulfill your holy will. Make us worthy to receive your blessings and mercies at all times, now and forever.[3]

THE GENEVAN PSALTER

Hughes Oliphant Old in his *The Patristic Roots of the Reformed Worship* mentions the rubrics of the prayer for illumination.[4] These rubrics appear in the Genevan Psalter of 1542. It gives us the following details regarding the reformed prayer for illumination:

> Then the minister commences again to pray, beseeching God for the Grace of His Holy Spirit, that His Word may be faithfully expounded to the honor of His name and the edification of the Church, and be received with such humility and obedience which it deserves, The form is left to the discernment of the minister.[5]

The exact wording of the prayer of illumination is not mentioned by Old. Brad Thompson's book *Liturgies of the Western Church*, which serves as Old's source only has the above mentioned rubrics.[6] This could be understood, because the prayer for illumination was an extempore prayer to be prayed by the minister. In this extempore prayer, the minister had to make sure that the above rubrics were covered.

Elsie Mckee provides us with a translated version of the wordings of the extempore "prayer for illumination-sealing."

> We call upon the heavenly Father, Father of all goodness and mercy, asking Him to cast the eye of His mercy on us His poor servants, not imputing to us the many faults and offenses we have committed, by which we have provoked His wrath against us, but [instead] seeing us

---

3. *Mar Thoma Church*, 42. *Malankara Mar Thoma*, 12–13.
4. Old, *Patristic Roots*, 208.
5. Old, *Patristic Roots*, 208.
6. Thompson, *Liturgies*, 198–99.

The Prayer for Illumination: Address and Petition

in the face of His Son, Jesus Christ our Lord, as He has established Him as Mediator between Him and us. Let us pray that, as the whole plentitude of wisdom and light is in Him, He may guide us by His Holy Spirit to the true understanding of His holy teaching, and may make it bear in us all the fruits of righteousness, to the glory and honor of His Name, and the instruction and edification of His church....[7]

A preliminary comparison of Mckee's translated prayer with the rubrics provided by Old reveals that there is one difference between the two. While Old indicates that the prayer is addressed to God, McKee's translation shows that in the address God the Father is called upon to look upon the worshipper through Jesus Christ. A closer look at the three prayers indicates that the prayer for illumination can be divided into four parts: address, petition, fruit, and doxology. A tabular comparison of the three prayers is as follows:

Table 1: Comparison of Prayer for illumination

	SYRIAN LITURGY	GENEVAN PSALTER (RUBRICS, Old)	GENEVAN PSALTER (PRAYER, McKee)	MAR THOMA LITURGY
ADDRESSED TO	Lord God	God	God the Father through Jesus Christ	Lord God
PETITION	To be filled with the understanding of the Holy Gospel	To receive the Word in humility and obedience	To be guided by the Holy Spirit in the true understanding of the holy teachings	To be filled with the truth of the Gospel

---

7. Calvin, *Writings on Pastoral Piety*, 112.

The Prayer of Illumination

	To be filled with the richness of the gifts of God		Acknowledges the plentitude of wisdom and light in God	To be filled with the riches of the Lord's holy wisdom
	To be filled with the grace of the Holy Spirit	To receive the grace of the Holy Spirit		To be filled with the gift of the Holy Spirit.
	To be given knowledge of divine words			To be given the knowledge and discernment of divine words
FRUIT	To be able to keep the commandments	To honor God's name	To glory and honor God's name	To joyfully follow the Lord's commandments
	To be able to accomplish the Lord's will	To edify the church	To instruct and edify God's church	To fully obey the will of God
	To be accounted worthy of the blessings, and the mercies from the Lord.		To bear the fruits of righteousness	To be made worthy to receive the blessings and mercies of God
DOXOLOGY	To Thee now and all times			At all times now and forever

The above table lays out a detailed comparison of the prayer for illumination from the three texts under consideration. The similarities and differences have to be further analyzed separately.

In this chapter I will cover the analysis of first two parts, i.e., the address and the petition.

The Prayer for Illumination: Address and Petition

A comparison of the Syrian Liturgy and the MTL from the table above shows that they are quite similar. Hence, in the following analysis the MTL and the Syrian liturgy are taken together. I will descriptively map and analyze the address first.

THE ADDRESS

As is evident in the table, the prayers of the Syrian Liturgy as well as the MTL are addressed to God. To address the prayer to "Lord God" can mean that the prayer is addressed only to God without any reference to the Triune God, or it can mean that the three persons of the Trinity are implicitly implied in the address to God. If the prayer was referring to any one person of the Trinity it would have explicitly said so. However, since the prayer is addressed to "Lord God," it is safe to conclude that the prayer is not explicitly addressed to any one person of the Trinity, but to the Triune God. The three persons of the Trinity, i.e., God the Father, God the Son, and God the Holy Spirit are implied in the address to God. This is also credible when we observe that most of the prayers of the Syrian Liturgy and the MTL end in a reference to the Triune God.[8]

Such an implicit reference in the *address* to the three persons of the Godhead would mean that to pray to God the Father is the same as to pray to God the Son or God the Holy Spirit. It would mean that there is an inherent unity of the Godhead implied by the address. Such an emphasis is also found in St. Basil who was instrumental in developing the address "Glory be to the Father, and to the Son, and to the Holy Spirit."[9] Through this usage, Basil is trying to emphasize the communion between the Father, the Son, and the Holy Spirit in such a way that one cannot be separated from another. The three are interconnected in communion with each other. Boris Bobrinskoy affirms this communion in Basil's *On*

---

8. *Mar Thoma Church*, 50, 52; *Anaphora*, 20, 25.
9. For a brief mention of the history see Edwards, *Breath of Life*, 22–23.

The Prayer of Illumination

the Holy Spirit, and states, "The key term in *On the Holy Spirit* is *Koinonia* (communion)."[10]

We can conclude that the address to "Lord God" in the Syrian Liturgy as well as the MTL implicitly points to a communion in the Godhead. It is a communion in which an address to any one person of the Godhead implies an address to all the three persons of the Godhead. In other words, to address the prayer for illumination to "Lord God" is an address to God the Father, God the Son, and God the Holy Spirit at the same time.

The prayer in the Genevan Psalter is addressed explicitly to God the Father. When an address is explicitly addressed to one particular person, the person who is addressed is expected to respond; a Triune reference is mentioned in the prayer. God the Father is asked to look in the face of His Son Jesus Christ, be merciful to the sinners, and send the Holy Spirit. The Triune reference brings out the function of each person of the Godhead. God the Father sees through Jesus and guides the worshipper in the Holy Spirit. This order makes sense when one understands that for Calvin Jesus Christ covers up the sin, and the Holy Spirit guides the worshipper in the "true understanding of [God's] holy teaching."[11]

Notice that the Genevan address can imply a functional difference in the Godhead, i.e., God the Father functions in sending the Holy Spirit, God the Son functions in covering up the sins of the people, and God the Holy Spirit functions in guiding the worshipper in the holy teachings. On a general note, when three different functions are assigned to three persons it means that the three persons will do it differently. However, there will be a unity in the way the task is carried out by the three persons. The three persons will be united in the objective and the purpose of the objective. Such a unity is present in the Godhead. It is a unity of purpose and objective. This is not to suggest that the three persons

---

10. Bobrinskoy, *Mystery of the Trinity*, 244. A detailed discussion on communion is beyond the scope of this book as it enters into discussion of the Triune nature of God. However, for a brief reading on communion of the Triune God, see Edwards, *Breath of Life*, 24–30.

11. Calvin, *Writings on Pastoral Piety*, 112.

The Prayer for Illumination: Address and Petition

of the Godhead are different and are only united in purpose and objective. It is clear that God the Father is called upon through the prayer for illumination to guide the worshipper through the Holy Spirit into the "true understanding of [God's] holy teaching."[12] We can arguably conclude that a Triune reference is attested in the address of the prayer for illumination. To make a detailed argument for the unity of the Godhead is beyond the scope of this book. However, I will endeavor to suggest a basic unity in the Godhead.

I suggested that a unity in purpose and objective in the Godhead is envisioned in the Genevan Psalter's prayer for illumination. However, we can establish an inherent unity in the Godhead through this prayer. Let us consider a case scenario involving three entities, i.e., X Y, and Z. X cannot guide another person, Y, into the understanding of a third person, Z. Since the mind of X, Y, and Z are different, they will understand a particular thing in different ways. The person X can convince the person Y to a large extent about the intention of Z. Now suppose if X is the Holy Spirit, Y is the worshipper, and Z is God the Father, then there is some distancing of some sort from the Holy Spirit, and from God the Father, if we apply the above stated relation between X, Y, and Z. However, the prayer for illumination presents before us a possibility where X is Z. Z (God the Father) is asked to send X (the Holy Spirit), who will guide the worshipper Y in the understanding of God's Holy teaching, i.e., the holy teaching of Z. For X to guide Y (the worshipper) in the teaching of Z (God the Father), the mind of X should be the same as that of Z. This is possible only if X is Z. The work of the Holy Spirit is to guide the worshipper in the understanding of God's holy teaching. Though I would not dwell more on this comparison, we can arguably conclude that to ask God the Father to send the Holy Spirit to guide the worshipper in God's Holy teaching, is to say that there is an inherent unity between God the Father and the Holy Spirit.

This is clear when we understand that Calvin evaluates the work of the Spirit, and concludes that the Holy Spirit is divine because the Holy Spirit's works point to divinity. The work of

---

12. Calvin, *Writings on Pastoral Piety*, 112.

The Prayer of Illumination

creation, preservation, the sending of the prophets, and the experience of godliness by humans, are all proof for Calvin that the Spirit is divine.[13] Referring to the Holy Spirit, Calvin says, "Upon him, as upon the Son, are conferred functions that especially belong to divinity."[14] Applying this understanding to the case of X, Y, and Z we can say that X (the Holy Spirit) is able to guide the worshipper in the holy teaching, because the Holy Spirit shares in the divinity of Z (God the Father). However, when we share something it could mean that the thing we share is not inherently ours and is probably given to us. If the Holy Spirit shares in the divinity of God the Father in this sense, it would mean that the Holy Spirit is not fully divine, but just shares in the divinity of God the Father in a secondary way.

To understand this divinity of the Holy Spirit we should understand as stated above that for Calvin the divinity is inferred from the functionality of the Holy Spirit. Thus, Calvin says, "For if Spirit were not an entity subsisting in God, choice and will would by no means be conceded to him."[15] Calvin says that the Holy Spirit can choose, and will, because the Holy Spirit "subsists" in God. Subsisting here takes the meaning of remaining in the being of God.[16] Remaining in the being of God means to be God in essence. For nothing can remain in one's being other than that which is fully one's own. It is this divine nature of remaining in the being of God that gives the Holy Spirit the freedom to choose and will. It is this divine nature that leads to the work of the Holy Spirit.

We can conclude that in the Syrian Liturgy, MTL, and the Genevan Psalter the address is Triune. Though in the Syrian Liturgy as well as the MTL an explicit Triune reference is not made in the address it cannot be ruled out. The Triune address in the Genevan Psalter points to an explicit unity of the Godhead in terms of the function, the purpose, the being, and the essence of Godhead.

---

13. Calvin, *Institutes*, 1.13.14, 138–39.
14. Calvin, *Institutes*, 1.13.14, 138–39.
15. Calvin, *Institutes*, 1.13.14, 138–39.
16. For a background of Calvin's use of the word "subsistence" see Calvin, *Institutes*, 1.13.14, 125–28.

The Prayer for Illumination: Address and Petition

In the address of the prayer for illumination, the MTL is eastern as well as reformed. It is eastern in the sense that the prayer is implicitly addressed to the Triune God. The explicit address to the Triune God in the prayer for illumination in the Genevan Psalter is similar to the implicit address to the Triune God in the prayer for illumination in the MTL. It is similar in the sense that a communion in the Godhead is suggested by the address. However, a functional difference is suggested by the address of the Genevan Psalter. This does not discredit the similarity of the MTL with the Syrian Liturgy and the Genevan Psalter.

Let us now start descriptively mapping and analyzing the petitions.

PETITION

Let us analyze the beginning of the petitions.

In terms of the petition there is a similarity in the three liturgies. All the three petitions ask either "to be filled" with the Holy Spirit (in case of Syrian and MTL), "to grant" (only Syrian Liturgy), or to "receive the grace" of the Holy Spirit (Genevan Psalter). First we will analyze the usages of "to fill," "to grant," and "to receive."

We will first analyze the usage "to be filled."

"To Fill," "to Grant," and "to Receive"

"To be filled" can imply the following possibilities:

1. The thing that is being filled is empty.
2. The thing that is being filled is not fully filled so it is filled in order to be fully filled.
3. The thing that is being filled is full to the brim, but it is still being filled irrespectively.

When the object that is being filled is a thing, then the above possibilities hold true. However, the prayer petitions Lord God for the worshippers "to be filled" with the Holy Spirit. So the object

The Prayer of Illumination

under consideration is not a thing, but rather people. More exactly, in liturgical tradition the petition comes under the section of prayers that are addressed to believers as well as unbelievers.[17] Gregory Dix calls this section of the liturgy "propaganda meetings," stating that it was meant for people who desired to be converted. Dix mentions that such meetings consisted of reading Scripture and oral instruction. In this meeting, those who were not baptized also attended, but the Eucharist that followed later was exclusively for the baptized. If the prayer was petitioned for unbelievers who were not baptized, we have to conclude that unbelievers would be totally devoid or not filled by the Holy Spirit. The first possibility holds good for the unbeliever who was not baptized. So "to be filled" can imply that the worshippers present do not have the filling of the Holy Spirit, and the prayer petitions God to fill those present in the worship with the Holy Spirit. It could be understood as a filling for the first time.

However, a closer study of the tradition would reveal that the believers also attended the service.[18] If it is believers who are in question, then the second and third possibilities hold true. A continuous filling is suggested by these two possibilities. A continuous filling is needed only when there is a necessity to be filled continually. If something is filled to the brim then we can say that further filling is not required. However, humans struggle with sin daily thus necessitating a need for the continuous filling of the Holy Spirit in order to live a Christian life.

Such a continuous filling is also indicated in the writings on Cyril of Jerusalem. Cyril, drawing from Prov 5:15 and John 4:14, compares the Holy Spirit to the living water, which fills up in the believer.[19] This would mean that the Holy Spirit indwells in us continuously. Such thought can also be found in Basil who, explaining Ps 35:10, refers to the Holy Spirit as the One within us

---

17. For a brief reading see Dix, *Shape of the Liturgy*, 16–17.

18. Dix, *Shape of the Liturgy*, 16–18. Whether the unbeliever or the believer is filled does not come under the scope of this thesis. The importance is given to the continuous filling of the Holy Spirit.

19. Cyril, "Catechetical Lectures," in *St. Cyril of Jerusalem*, xvi.11, 117.

The Prayer for Illumination: Address and Petition

who enlightens and illuminates us to see the true light which is Jesus.[20] Thus, the Holy Spirit fills the worshipper with light so that the worshipper is able to grow spiritually. This indwelling of the Spirit led Gregory Nazianzus to write, "It is the Spirit in whom we worship, and in whom we pray."[21]

We can conclude that the usage of "to be filled" with the Holy Spirit, which is found in the Syrian and the MTL, are in line with the teaching of the eastern fathers. The phrase "to be filled" conveys a dependency on the Holy Spirit to live the Christian life. The Syrian and the MTL bring to fore the human nature as frail and in dire need of the filling of the Holy Spirit. The Holy Spirit is sought to dwell in us to help us to grow spiritually in Jesus Christ.

The Syrian Liturgy has an additional usage, i.e., "to grant."

The usage "to grant" means that something that belongs wholly to someone else is asked to be granted. The phrase "to grant" something to someone entails a conditionality on the part of the giver and a limitation on the part of the receiver. The conditionality on the part of the giver has to be met for the grant to be given. The one who is receiving it has to make use of the thing being granted within a framework of rules that governs the thing being granted. Hence the receiver is bonded to the giver. This would mean that the receiver does not have the freedom to use the thing being granted according to his or her wish. The one who is granting has a claim over the thing being granted. However, the one who is receiving the grant has to cooperate with the condition on which the grant is given. Even though the receiver is limited by th laws governing the grant, the receiver has to oblige and make the grant effective.

So when the worshipper prays to God to grant the knowledge, it means that the worshipper will be governed by the knowledge that is granted. However, the worshipper has to cooperate with the knowledge that God grants. It is this cooperation that makes the knowledge effective. The worshipper is governed by the laws of this knowledge. However, following the granting of this

---

20. Špidlík, *Spirituality of the Christian East*, 33.
21. Nazianzen, "Fifth Theological Oration," in *St. Cyril of Jerusalem*, 321.

The Prayer of Illumination

knowledge, the worshipper starts cooperating with the knowledge that is granted.

We can conclude that in contrast to the MTL the Syrian Liturgy suggests that the knowledge granted through the prayer for illumination governs the worshipper in understanding the divine words. The illumination elevates the capacity of the worshipper to make choices to accept the knowledge that is granted. Consequently, the worshipper starts cooperating with the knowledge that is granted.

The usage in the Genevan Psalter, i.e., "to receive," can imply the following possibilities:

1. The thing that is received is either given freely or not freely.
2. The thing that is received is given freely for a purpose.
3. The thing that is received is instrumental in achieving the purpose.

The act of giving something requires the consent of the receiver. Without the consent of the receiver, the thing that is given will have no relevance. The receiver has to accept the thing that is given, for the received thing to be made of use by the receiver. It would mean that the receiver can disregard the thing given as a result of which the affectivity of the thing that is given would be stalled. However, the prayer for illumination is prayed by the worshipper. This would mean that the worshipper of his or her own consent asks to be given the Holy Spirit. Since the worshipper asks for the Holy Spirit, the onus is on God to give the Holy Spirit. Scripture testifies to the free gift of the Holy Spirit.[22] We can say that the Holy Spirit is given freely.

Furthermore, when something is received, it would mean that it is given to the receiver for a purpose. The prayer for illumination anticipates that the Holy Spirit is given for a purpose. Such a gift would mean that the Holy Spirit is the means toward an end. If the Holy Spirit is understood as a means towards an end, then it would follow that the Holy Spirit could be disposed of and be substituted

---

22. Luke 24:49; John 14:26.

The Prayer for Illumination: Address and Petition

by any other means. Such an understanding of the Holy Spirit is not promoted by the prayer for illumination. The Holy Spirit is looked upon not as a secondary means, but as a requirement on the part of humans to achieve a desired purpose. So the Holy Spirit is not a means in the traditional understanding. The Holy Spirit cannot be disposed of, and without the gift of the Holy Spirit the purpose cannot be achieved. If the Holy Spirit cannot be disposed of, then the Holy Spirit is intimately and intrinsically related to human life.

Such a relation of the Holy Spirit to the Christian life is evident in Calvin, for whom the Holy Spirit is the "bond by which Christ effectually unites us to Himself."[23] A bond is something that unites two entities. The purpose of uniting is to maintain the bond. However, without the bond the two entities cannot coexist. Hence, the bond is a necessary prerequisite.

We can conclude that the Holy Spirit is given freely to the worshipper. The Holy Spirit is given for a purpose. The purpose is to maintain the communion with God. The active agent in the worshipper working toward the purpose of God is the Holy Spirit. The Genevan Psalter gives emphasis to the agency of the Holy Spirit. The MTL is eastern and reformed in suggesting a dependency on the Holy Spirit to live the Christian life. The MTL is not eastern in the sense that it does not go on to convey that after the knowledge that is granted through illumination of the Holy Spirit, the worshipper starts cooperating with the Holy Spirit and effects the understanding of the divine words. It is neither fully reformed in stating that the Holy Spirit is the only active agent in the worshipper. We can say that the MTL suggests a working of the Holy Spirit vis-a-vis with the cooperation of the worshipper. The worshipper is not controlled fully by the operation of illumination of the Holy Spirit. The cooperation of the worshipper is also not what controls the affectivity of the illumination of the Holy Spirit.

Let us now analyze the main body of the petition. We will break down the main body of the petition into the following

---

23. Calvin, *Institutes*, 3.1.1, 531.

sub-sections: knowledge of God, divine words, holiness of God, and truth, wisdom of God, and illumination.

Knowledge of God

The words that signify a petition for the knowledge of God are: *To be given the knowledge and discernment* (MTL); *to be granted the knowledge* (Syrian Liturgy); *to receive the Word in humility and obedience* (rubrics of Genevan Psalter).

Webster's online dictionary defines knowledge as a "state of being aware of something."[24] Discernment can be understood as the ability to perceive or understand. This ability to perceive involves the process of understanding and making choices based on what is understood. It means that the mind and the will is at work in coming to a decision on what is discerned. We can say that discernment involves a process. Once a person is being made aware of something, then the next step for the person is to discern what is being known. Hence discernment is a process of growing in knowledge. So discernment can be categorized under knowledge.

Moreover, knowledge is always acquired as opposed to inborn. Nobody is born knowledgeable; rather, everybody grows in knowledge day by day. The process of acquiring knowledge is either by education, by experience, by observation, or by a skill. In all the above instances knowledge is acquired by an active participation by the human person. Once the person acquires a basic skill set or education the person can use that knowledge to grow further in knowledge. So we can say that a primary knowledge, for example an education in science, is acquired through the above mentioned process. This primary knowledge then serves as the foundation for further knowledge.

However, the prayer for illumination is prayed every time before the Gospel is read within the liturgy. Applying the definition of knowledge, we could say that the worshipper prays for knowledge by which the worshipper is made aware of something

---

24. Merriam-Webster Online Dictionary, "Knowledge."

The Prayer for Illumination: Address and Petition

inherent in the Gospel. This is the basic or primary knowledge to understand the Gospel. As the worshipper prays for such knowledge to be given, it would mean that this knowledge is different from the primary knowledge acquired in the world. This would mean that the knowledge prayed for in the prayer cannot be compared with the primary knowledge that a person acquires due to some education or experience. If the knowledge that is prayed for is not the primary knowledge then the knowledge or discernment prayed for in the prayer for illumination should be new each time the Gospel is read. If the knowledge is new it would also mean that the knowledge cannot be acquired by the way in which the knowledge of the world is acquired. It would mean that the knowledge or discernment required to understand the Gospel is something not of this world, but rather spiritual. Such a spiritual knowledge is implanted in the worshipper as a result of the prayer for illumination. Hence the prayer for illumination suggests that it is not possible to know the divine words through the natural knowledge.

Such an aspect of God's unknowability by the human faculties is also suggested by Gregory of Nazianzus who maintains that God is incomprehensible and cannot be fully known.[25] This is a recurring theme in Gregory's *Oration* 28, thereby underlining that God cannot be grasped by human understanding.[26] For Gregory, it is the inability of the creatures to understand in entirety the creator of all things. We can argue that God can be known through God's work. However, for Gregory this knowledge about God that is derived from the work of God is incomplete. For Gregory, the knowledge about the fullness of God's being, i.e., the knowledge of who or what God is, is not fully known from the works of God. The above case can also be extended to the words of God or divine words. If the knowledge of God is incomprehensible on the pretext that the limited human mind cannot comprehend the limitless

---

25. Nazianzen, "Second Theological Oration," in *St. Cyril of Jerusalem*, 288–94.

26. Nazianzen, "Second Theological Oration," in *St. Cyril of Jerusalem*, 288–94.

God, then the knowledge of God's word is also incomprehensible on the very same pretext.

We can conclude that the prayer for illumination of the MTL suggests that a worshipper acquires a basic or primary knowledge from the world. This knowledge can be categorized as *natural* knowledge. However, through this *natural* knowledge it is not possible to know God. As opposed to this, a *spiritual* knowledge is implanted because of the prayer for illumination, in order to understand the divine words. The MTL is eastern in the sense that it agrees with the eastern fathers on the unknowability of God's words. However, the prayer for illumination in the MTL brings in the aspect of discernment, which includes a process of choice and decision on the part of the worshipper. The agency of the Holy Spirit is actively working with the agency of the human. As against this, I argued that the usage of "to grant" in the Syrian Liturgy suggests that the worshipper after the illumination cooperates with the work of the Holy Spirit.

In the rubrics of Genevan Psalter as suggested by Old, the worshipper petitions "to receive the Word in humility and obedience." We have already discussed the usage of "to receive." The inclusion of "humility and obedience" underlines the attitude that the worshipper should have when the Word is received. It also suggests that there is a possibility for the worshipper to be proud and disobedient. In the context of the prayer for illumination the worshipper can be thought to be proud when the worshipper is in possession of something more worthy than the Word that is to be received. Since the Word that is to be received has to do with knowledge, the only thing that the worshipper would be proud of is his or her knowledge as opposed to the knowledge of the Word received. Similarly, for the worshipper to be disobedient to the Word that is received, it would mean that the worshipper is involved in a process of comparing and deciding whether to accept the Word that is received. In both the cases, i.e., humility and obedience, the capacity of the worshipper to be proud and disobedient toward the Word that is to be received is taken into consideration. In this

The Prayer for Illumination: Address and Petition

context the worshipper through the prayer for illumination prays for humility and obedience toward the Word that is to be received. When we consider Calvin, we see that he begins his *Institutes* with the famous lines "nearly all the wisdom we possess, that is to say, true and sound wisdom, consists of two parts: the knowledge of God and of ourselves."[27] A demarcation is made between two types of knowledge. Calvin proceeds to argue that knowledge of ourselves leads to a realization of human finitude, which in turn leads us to the "true light of wisdom [which] rests in the Lord alone."[28] He further says that "the knowledge of ourselves not only arouses us to seek God, but also, as it were, leads us by the hand to find him."[29] So Calvin starts with something that is known to us, i.e., human reality, and comes to a conclusion that it should compel us to know the unknown. This process of knowing necessarily involves comparing the natural knowledge with the spiritual knowledge. As a result of this comparison a decision is reached on the part of the believer.

Calvin wants us to understand that "there is within the human mind, and indeed by the natural instinct, an awareness of divinity."[30] This sort of awareness of the divine is "implanted" by God himself. We should not mistake Calvin as advocating that we can know God or God's words through the human intellect. Calvin goes on to declare that to know God through our intellect is "empty speculation."[31] This would mean that whatever humans have come to know of God through their effort is a partial knowledge of God. For Calvin the Holy Spirit illumines the worshipper and the true knowledge of God "takes root in the heart"[32] of the worshipper. The work of God in creation touches the heart and evokes an already implanted basic knowledge of God to grow continuously.

27. Calvin, *Institutes*, 1.1.1, 35.
28. Calvin, *Institutes*, 1.1.1, 36.
29. Calvin, *Institutes*, 1.1.1, 37.
30. Calvin, *Institutes*, 1.3.1, 43.
31. Calvin, *Institutes*, 1.5.9, 61–62.
32. Calvin, *Institutes*, 1.5.9, 62.

The Prayer of Illumination

In contrast to Gregory of Nazianzus for whom human or anything finite cannot be a starting point to know God, Calvin advocates a knowing of God with human realities as the starting point. Both of them agree that we can know God to some extent through God's work. Calvin acknowledges that humans involve in a process of comparing and deciding on the knowledge received. This process of comparison and decision can lead us to proudness and disobedience toward the divine knowledge. In order to avoid this, the worshipper prays "to receive the word in humility and obedience."

We can conclude that the prayer for illumination of the Syrian, the MTL, and the Genevan Psalter points to the limitation to the human capacity to know God. The MTL is eastern and reformed in this sense. However, the prayer for illumination of the MTL and the Genevan Psalter does recognize the human capacity to think, compare, and decide. The prayer gives some consideration to the human capacity to know through its own natural faculties. The MTL is reformed in this sense. For Calvin this natural capacity of humans can lead to only a partial knowledge of God. As a result of this natural capacity humans can become proud and disobedient toward the Word that is to be received. The prayer for illumination of the MTL does not suggest such possibility. The MTL is not reformed in this sense.

The prayer for illumination in the Genevan Psalter suggests that illumination of the Holy Spirit implants the true knowledge of God in the worshipper. Hence, theologically the Genevan Psalter sets the natural knowledge in contrast to the knowledge received through the Spirit. This natural knowledge has to be superseded by the spiritual knowledge. The prayers for illumination in all three liturgies unite in the petition to be "filled by," "to grant," or "to receive" the Holy Spirit. All three prayers acknowledge that knowledge of divine words has its source in the divine Being, i.e., God. Hence, a spiritual discernment is needed. Since the knowledge and discernment is spiritual, a prayer is required for the knowledge or discernment to be "given" (MTL) or "granted" (Syrian Liturgy) or "received" (Genevan Psalter). The worshipper prays to the Lord

The Prayer for Illumination: Address and Petition

God to give such a knowledge or discernment. It is explicitly spiritual knowledge, because the knowledge or discernment under consideration is either that of the "divine words" (Mar Thoma and Syrian) or of the "Word" (Genevan Psalter).

Divine Words

The words that signify a petition discernment of the divine words are: *To be given the knowledge and discernment of divine words* (MTL); *to be granted the knowledge of God's divine words* (Syrian Liturgy); *to receive the Word in humility and obedience* (rubrics of Genevan Psalter).

The phrase "divine words" means that the words are not human. Hence, divine words can be given only by God. "Words" could imply the Scripture portions that are being read before and after the prayer of illumination. In that case it would cover the whole of Scripture. Since this prayer for illumination is followed by the reading of the Gospel, it would be safe to presume that the prayer for illumination refers to the knowledge or discernment of the words read in the Gospel portion.

If the prayer for illumination refers to the Gospel portion, then the question we have to ask is: what is so different in the Gospel portion that cannot be understood by a normal reading or hearing of the Gospel? Since the Gospel portion that is being read is composed of intelligible words, it should be understandable. However, as we discussed in the preceding section the prayer for illumination suggests that something more than intelligence is present in the words of the Gospel. A knowledge that is different than the knowledge of the world is present in the divine words read from the Gospel. Such a knowledge that is present in the divine words of the Gospel portion can only be understood if somebody who is divine helps us. We can conclude that God who is divine helps us through the illumination of the Holy Spirit in gaining knowledge and discernment that is not just intelligible to the human mind, but that is above all spiritually known and discerned by the worshipper. God gives us the knowledge and discernment to understand the spiritual knowledge of the divine words.

The divine words, referring to the Gospel portion, could refer either to the words of Jesus or to the words that describe the life and events of Jesus. The qualifier "divine" is especially important because it establishes that divine words refer to the life and events of Jesus. It follows that these divine words are of special importance. Gregory of Nazianzus also emphasizes an underlying meaning to the actual written words of Scripture. For him, there is an "inner meaning" and a "hidden beauty," which is "irradiated by the light of knowledge."[33] We can say that the words of the Gospel have an "inner meaning." The worshipper knows this inner meaning after the illumination of the Holy Spirit.

The words of the Gospel can be said to be important on the following grounds:

1. They convey either the words or the events associated with Jesus.
2. They are one of the first writings of the early church.
3. They convey the commandments of Jesus for the church.

All the above three possibilities are associated either with Jesus or with the New Testament church, which was a result of the life and events associated with Jesus. When we look to Gregory of Nazianzus, we see an attitude of reverence and necessity of the Gospel in his writings. The necessity of the Gospel for Gregory stems from the fact that in the Gospel, Jesus is revealed as the second person of the Godhead.[34] Cyril of Jerusalem also expresses a harmony in the whole Scriptures.[35] The harmony has to do with how the Scriptures testify about Christ. Thus Cyril says:

---

33. Nazianzen, "Fifth Theological Oration," in *St. Cyril of Jerusalem*, 21, 324.

34. Nazianzen, "Fifth Theological Oration," in *St. Cyril of Jerusalem*, 324–25, 338–44.

35. Cyril, "First Catechetical Lecture," in *St. Cyril of Jerusalem*, 9.

The Prayer for Illumination: Address and Petition

For the things concerning Christ are all put into writing, and nothing is doubtful, for nothing is without a text. All are inscribed on the monuments of the prophets; clearly written, not on tablets of stone, but by the Holy Ghost.[36]

Notice here that for Cyril it is undoubtedly Christ who brings importance to the Gospel portion of Scripture, but this happens through the Holy Spirit. There is an understanding of the words of the Scripture being written by the Holy Spirit.[37] By this, Cyril means that the Holy Spirit was at work when the Scriptures were written. Hence, to understand the Scripture the Holy Spirit is needed. For Cyril the words of the Scripture are sealed in the heart through the Holy Spirit.[38]

We can conclude that for the eastern fathers, although the Scripture radiates the message about Christ, the Gospel stands out as an immediate witness to the life and events of Jesus. The life and witness of the church are inseparable from the life and events associated with Jesus. The prayer for illumination of the MTL is eastern in the sense that it acknowledges that since the Holy Spirit was instrumental in shaping the Gospel, the Holy Spirit alone can guide the worshipper to the inner meaning of the divine words, i.e., the Gospels. The inner meaning of the Gospel has to do with Christ who is proclaimed through the Gospels. God gives us the knowledge and discernment to understand the spiritual knowledge of the divine words. This knowledge and discernment is given through the illumination of the Holy Spirit. The divine words are sealed in the heart of the hearers through the Holy Spirit.

So should we say that through the reading of the Gospel the presence of Jesus is made real in worship? Surely the church has the promise of Jesus to claim the presence of Jesus.[39] However, to what degree this presence is made real or present through the Gospel reading is unclear. It is not suggested by the prayer for

---

36. Cyril, "First Catechetical Lecture," in *St. Cyril of Jerusalem*, 84.
37. Cyril, "First Catechetical Lecture," in *St. Cyril of Jerusalem*, 86.
38. Cyril, "First Catechetical Lecture," in *St. Cyril of Jerusalem*, 86.
39. Matt 18:20: "Where two or three are gathered in my name there am I among them."

illumination. However, when we consider this question with the petition of the Genevan Psalter, i.e., "to receive the Word" (rubrics as specified by Old), new possibilities emerge.

In comparison to the prayer for illumination in the Mar Thoma and Syrian liturgy where "divine words" are used, in the Genevan Psalter "the Word" is used. Whenever the definite article "the" is used, it specifies a particular thing. This specification given by the definite article implies that the thing specified is very important or has a special value. On the contrary, when an indefinite article "a" or "an" is used, it has a generalizing effect on what is specified. So the usage "receive *the* Word" means that the thing that is specified, i.e., Word, is of special importance.

We could further say that the definite article "the" points to the uniqueness of "Word." It is interesting to notice that the capital letter "W" is used for "Word." When a capital letter is used it focuses attention on a particular entity within any group of people, places, things, etc. The usage "the Word" could suggest a particular word among the words that are spoken in the Gospel reading or it could suggest the biblical witness of Jesus, the "Word incarnate."[40] The possibility of referring to a particular word in the Gospel reading is not possible as a capital W is used in "Word." This leaves us with the possibility that Jesus the Word incarnate is referred to in the usage "to receive the Word."

However, when we analyze the rubrics as specified by Old with the actual prayer as specified by McKee[41] we see that no such mention is present in the actual prayer. Rather the prayer reads, "Let us pray that, as the whole plentitude of wisdom, and light is in Him, He may guide us by His Holy Spirit to the true understanding of His holy teaching." There is no mention of "receiving the Word." On the contrary, the Holy Spirit is asked to guide the worshipper in the holy teachings as the Gospel is read. Thus it is not possible to arrive at a conclusion that the Word refers to the presence of Jesus. The prayer as specified by McKee makes sense

---

40. John 1:1.
41. Calvin, *Writings on Pastoral Piety*, 112.

The Prayer for Illumination: Address and Petition

when we understand Calvin's approach toward Scripture and the Gospels.

For Calvin, Scripture is the "light of [God's] Word... a direct and more certain mark whereby [God] is to be recognized."[42] For Calvin, Scripture has been given by God to help us in our salvation. Scripture helps to disperse the "confused knowledge of God in our minds" and to show us clearly "the true God."[43] Notice here that Calvin identifies a basic knowledge in the human mind. This knowledge, he maintains, confuses the knowledge about the true God. In order to have the true knowledge of the true God, the hearing of the Scripture is necessary. Calvin goes on to expound Jer 31:31–34, saying that the Gospel is spiritual in character and is "written upon men's heart" by the "working of the Spirit."[44] Here we find a similar line of thought with the eastern fathers, for whom the hearing of the Gospel is sealed in the heart of the hearers by the Holy Spirit.

We can conclude that in the MTL, the Syrian Liturgy, and the Genevan Psalter, Scripture reading implants a spiritual knowledge that is different from the knowledge of the world. The Gospel reading is important because of the life and events of Christ in it. The words of the Gospel have to be sealed in the hearts of the hearers through the Holy Spirit. For a spiritual knowledge or discernment to be made possible, a prayer for illumination is needed. This spiritual knowledge and discernment enables the worshipper to understand the inner meaning of the Gospel. This inner meaning has to do with Christ and the events associated with Christ. We can say that the knowledge and discernment of [the] divine words, i.e., the words of the Gospel, are important for the life and sustenance of the church. Such a knowledge and discernment, which is more than just intelligible words, but rather spiritual words, is petitioned by the worshippers in the prayer for illumination. The MTL is eastern and reformed in the above sense.

---

42. Calvin, *Institutes*, 1.6.1, 69–70.
43. Calvin, *Institutes*, 1.6.1, 70.
44. Calvin, *Institutes*, 1.11.7–8, 456–57.

The Prayer of Illumination

Holiness of the Gospel and Truth

The words that signify a petition to understand the holy Gospel are: *To be filled with the truth of the holy Gospel* (MTL); *to be filled with the understanding of the holy Gospel* (Syrian Liturgy); *to be guided in the true understanding of the holy teachings* (Prayer of Genevan Psalter).

"Truth," as referred to in the MTL, points to something definite. "Understanding," as referred to in Syrian Liturgy, has to do with *how* a person perceives the truth. The thing that the person perceives can lead to the whole truth about the thing that is being perceived. Thus, understanding refers to a process of coming to know the whole truth. Thus truth, as used in the MTL, can mean that the worshipper has to reach the goal of knowing *the* truth rather than just the perception of the truth. Understanding, as used in the Syrian Liturgy, points to the process of reaching this goal. Thus, through a process of understanding and perceiving the different aspects of the truth, the worshipper comes to know *the* truth. The prayer for illumination of the MTL does not have an explicit mention of a process of understanding the different aspects of the truth in order to know *the* truth. However, such a process of knowing the truth is implicitly implied in the prayer.

Such an aspect of searching for the truth is found in the writings of St. Basil, who writes:

> To count the terms used in theology as of primary importance, and to endeavor to trace out the hidden meaning in every phrase and in every syllable, is a characteristic wanting in those who are idle in the pursuit of true religion. . . .[45]

Basil further writes that "truth is always a quarry hard to hunt, and therefore we must look everywhere for its tracks."[46] Athanasius, commenting on the nature of the truth, says that an "imperfect shadow of the truth [exists in our] conception."[47] Here

---

45. Basil, "On the Holy Spirit," 2.
46. Basil, "On the Holy Spirit," 2.
47. Athanasius, "Against the Heathen," in *St. Athanasius*, 563.

The Prayer for Illumination: Address and Petition

truth refers to the way we understand the divinity of the Word, i.e., Jesus Christ. Nevertheless, it brings out the difference between the real truth and some understanding of the real truth that exists in us. So Athanasius says a "perfect apprehension of the truth is at present far removed" from humans due to the "infirmity of the flesh."[48]

We can conclude that for the eastern fathers, truth is something for which one searches. The MTL is eastern in the sense a search for the truth is implied in its prayer for illumination.

The petition in the Genevan Psalter reads, "to be guided in the true understanding." It suggests that there is also a false understanding in which the worshipper can be guided into. This is made clear when we understand that for Calvin it is only in the elect that the knowledge of the holy Gospel is "imbued." For Calvin the nature of the truth is deeply connected to faith. In his distinction between the elect and the reprobate, Calvin maintains that truth reveals itself only in the elect. The truth of the Gospel endures eternally in the elect. Though the reprobate is touched by the "knowledge of [God's] gospel," over time this knowledge fades away. In the elect, the Spirit of God works to make sure that the knowledge of the gospel endures forever. So for Calvin the "true understanding of the Gospel" will be revealed only to the elect.[49] For Calvin, only the elect will be guided in the true understanding of the Gospel. The prayer for the Mar Thoma does not suggest such a distinction between the reprobate and the elect. Nevertheless, the process of guiding the elect in the true understanding of the Gospel involves perceiving different aspect of the truth and obtaining the true understanding.

We can conclude that the prayer for illumination of the MTL is not reformed in that it does not specify who will be guided into the true understanding of the holy Gospel. The Genevan Psalter has an underlying theological notion that only the elect will be guided into the true understanding of the holy Gospel. However, the prayer for illumination of the MTL is reformed in that it also

---

48. Athanasius, "Against the Heathen," in *St. Athanasius*, 563.
49. Calvin, *Institutes*, 3.2.12, 556–57.

suggests a process of being guided into the true understanding of the holy Gospel.

The question that we need to ask now is: how does a Gospel reading that consists of words read out loud become holy? As I argued before, the Gospel has a special place and importance owing to the content of the Gospel, i.e., the life and events associated with Jesus. However, when the adjective *holy* is added to the word *Gospel*, it elevates the Gospel to a higher plane. Holy can be understood as against unholy. To be holy means to be sacred or divine. The understanding of sacred connects one to God. A person is called holy when the person exhibits a great degree of relation with God or exhibits godly attributes. Thus, it is in relation to God that a person is called holy. Thus, the holiness of the person is an effect that is produced by a primary cause, i.e., God. In being the effect, the holiness is dependent on something else, rather than being free in itself. To be dependent in this sense is to be acted upon to produce holiness, and as such the holiness is *given*. So we can conclude that the holiness of the Gospel is due to three possible causes:

1. It is acted upon by God and made holy;
2. It is the content of the Gospel that makes it holy;
3. It is holy by itself.

The first and the second options may seem to be more agreeable as compared to the third. To say that the Gospel is holy in and of itself is to elevate the Gospel or in other words the Scripture to a divine status. Since Scripture testifies that "all scripture is God-breathed," what could stop the Gospel to be elevated to a divine status? We can also argue that it is also the content or the source of the Gospel, i.e., God, which makes the Gospel holy. We can conclude that the prayer for illumination is a prayer that helps the worshipper to understand the truth of the holy Gospel in the ways as stated above. Such a purpose of the prayer takes us to the next stage of the prayer.

The Prayer for Illumination: Address and Petition

Holy Wisdom

The words that signify a petition for holy wisdom are: *To be filled with the riches of the Lord's holy wisdom* (MTL); *to be filled with the riches of the gifts of God* (Syrian Liturgy); *as the whole plentitude of wisdom and light is in Him, He may guide us by His Holy Spirit to the true understanding of His holy teaching* (Genevan Psalter).

In order to understand the truth of the holy Gospel the worshipper petitions to be filled with the "holy wisdom" (MTL) or the "gifts of God" (Syrian Liturgy). In the Genevan Psalter a reference is made to the wisdom of God. In the light of this wisdom the worshipper petitions God to be guided by God's Holy Spirit to the true understanding of his holy teaching.

Wisdom can be understood as the quality of having a good judgment, perception, or understanding. When we say that somebody is wise, we reach that conclusion depending on the action that the concerned person takes. Hence, wisdom becomes a conclusion we reach as a result of a particular observation about a particular person. We can say that we reach at such a conclusion because the person has developed the quality through experience. Such a wisdom is always measured by the standards of the world, i.e., good and right as is understood in the world.

However, the wisdom that is petitioned for in the prayer is different than that which is seen in the world. The Scriptures also testify toward the existence of two types of wisdom.[50] The wisdom of the world can be understood by the human faculties on intelligible terms. However, the wisdom of God cannot be fully understood by the human faculties.[51] The worshipper petitions for this wisdom of God in the prayer for illumination. Since the source of this is God, the seeking of such wisdom will help the worshipper to understand the truth of the holy Gospel as the holiness of the Gospel is also dependent on God.

Such a distinction between two types of wisdom is also found in the writings of Basil, who differentiates between worldly

50. Jas 3:13–18.
51. 1 Cor 1:25.

The Prayer of Illumination

wisdom and godly wisdom. Worldly wisdom "willfully shut their eyes to the knowledge of the truth."[52] For Basil, the wisdom of God is "ineffable."[53] In other words, it is indescribable. The worshipper petitions for this wisdom of God that is indescribable and not understandable. Gregory of Nazianzus speaks of the wisdom and knowledge of God as hidden.[54] For Gregory of Nazianzus the Godly wisdom is not accessible by the natural mind. Such a knowing beyond that of the intellectual faculty suggests that there is some degree of unknowability when it comes to the wisdom of God. However, for Gregory of Nazianzus, when the person is enlightened by the Holy Spirit, the person will know the wisdom of God.[55]

For Calvin, the wisdom of God is "lofty" and helps us to "conceive God and what is God's."[56] However, for this the human mind had to be "illumined by the Spirit of God."[57] Drawing upon various Scriptural sources, Calvin says that the mind of humans "can become spiritually wise only in so far as God illumines it."[58] Calvin, drawing upon Pauline epistles, says that human wisdom is like a "veil that hinders the mind from seeing God."[59] Thus, the natural wisdom of humans cannot understand the heavenly wisdom of God.

We can conclude that the worshipper petitions for the wisdom of God so as to supersede or overcome natural wisdom of humans, which cannot understand the things of God. This is necessary to understand the truth of the holy Gospel. Such a holy wisdom enlightens the worshipper. The prayer for illumination in the MTL is eastern and reformed as it maintains a distinction between worldly wisdom and godly wisdom. The godly wisdom is beyond the understanding of the natural mind. Hence, the worshipper

---

52. Basil, *Hexaemeron*, 54.
53. Basil, *Hexaemeron*, 75.
54. Nazianzen, *St. Cyril of Jerusalem*, 70.
55. Nazianzen, *St. Cyril of Jerusalem*, 70.
56. Calvin, *Institutes*, 2.2.19, 278.
57 Calvin, *Institutes*, 2.2.19, 278.
58. Calvin, *Institutes*, 2.2.20, 279.
59. 1 Cor 1:13, 20.

The Prayer for Illumination: Address and Petition

seeks the help of the Holy Spirit to fill him or her with the holy wisdom.

When we analyze the Syrian Liturgy we see that it has the words "gifts of God." Gift means something that is given to another person freely. The act of giving the gift does not depend upon the consent of the receiver. The receiver can reject the gift. However, the gift is given irrespectively to the receiver, keeping in mind the receiver's benefit or happiness. However, in this prayer the receiver, i.e., the worshippers, are asking for the gift. The act of asking does not discredit the nature of the gift as free. When a person asks for a gift it could mean two things. First, that the person is demanding the gift against the desires of the giver. Second, the person is asking for the gift, because the person knows that he or she is receiving the gift because of the love of the giver. In the second sense it becomes not a demand, but rather seeking something in love. So we can conclude that the gifts of God are sought knowing that God freely gives God's gifts to his children.[60]

However, worldly gifts are perishable in nature. They are perishable because the gifts are made up of perishable things. In contrast to worldly gifts, the gifts of God are not perishable because they are spiritual in nature. The effects of the gifts are visible in tangible ways, for example, a person showing love. One can argue that such effects perish with the person's will to affect it or not. However, the gift of God cannot perish in and of itself even though the effect can or cannot perish depending on the person's accountability to the gift. The worshipper is filled with the riches of the gifts of God after the illumination of the Holy Spirit. The gift will always be there with the worshipper in a spiritual way. Such an intangible or spiritual nature of the gifts of God helps the worshipper to understand and know the truth of the holy Gospel, which is also spiritual. However, the Syrian Liturgy suggests that it is up to the worshipper to decide whether to use the gift.

Though the worshipper does not pray for wisdom explicitly in the Syrian Liturgy, it cannot be excluded from the gift of God. We can say that wisdom comes closest to be the probable gift, as an

---

60. Rom 8:32.

understanding of the truth of the holy Gospel is sought for. However, the gift of God can include a lot of things other than wisdom. It can include the gifts of the Holy Spirit. Hence, we can say that the worshipper prays for gifts of God other than wisdom.

We can conclude that in the Syrian Liturgy the worshipper asks for the gift of God to understand the truth of the holy Gospel. It is up to the worshipper to decide whether to use the gift. This gift includes the wisdom of God and also other gifts of God. The prayer for illumination of the MTL is not eastern in this sense.

Illumination

The words that signify a petition for the gift of the Holy Spirit are: *To be filled with the gift of the Holy Spirit* (MTL); *to be filled with the grace of the Holy Spirit* (Syrian Liturgy); *to receive the grace of the Holy Spirit* (Genevan Psalter).

It will be helpful to bear in mind the conclusion that we reached from treating the usage of "to fill" and "to receive." The active agent involved in the filling is the Holy Spirit. Without the Holy Spirit, the filling or receiving is not achievable. This is necessary to maintain the communion of the worshipper with God.

Furthermore, the mention of *Holy* as it appears here has a different connotation than the holy that appears before Gospel and wisdom. The *H* is capital here as compared to the lower case *h* used in the case of "wisdom" and "Gospel." So here *Holy* is not referring to a quality, but rather to the third person of the Trinity. The prayer for illumination that is addressed to God explicitly petitions for the gift or grace of the Holy Spirit.

The use of the conjunction "and"[61] in the prayer for illumination would mean that it conjoins the parts of the sentence. It

---

61. "Grant us, o Lord God, the knowledge of Thy divine words, and fill us with the understanding of Thy holy Gospel, and the richness of Thy divine gifts *and* the grace of thy Holy Spirit" (Syrian Liturgy). "[O Lord God,] give to us knowledge and discernment of your divine word(s). Fill us with the truth of your holy Gospel, the riches of your [holy] wisdom *and* the gift of your [Holy] Spirit" (MTL).

The Prayer for Illumination: Address and Petition

conveys an interconnectivity that cannot be done away with. If we substitute the conjunction *or* instead of *and* in the above liturgical prayer it would mean that either the "holy wisdom" or the "holy Gospel" or the "Holy Spirit" is petitioned for. The conjunction *or* is used to link alternatives, and that is where the importance of *and* comes in. The usage of *and* in the prayer for illumination brings out the importance that one cannot be separated from another. The three, i.e, *holy Gospel, holy wisdom*, and *Holy Spirit* are not alternatives for each other, but rather interconnected with one another.

It is important to dwell on the nature of this interconnection. We established in the preceding sections that the knowledge, discernment, and holy wisdom helps the worshipper in understanding the spiritual truth of the holy Gospel. However, it is obvious that knowledge, discernment, and holy wisdom itself cannot help the worshipper toward this end. If knowledge, discernment, and holy wisdom are to be effective in guiding the worshipper toward the spiritual truth of the holy Gospel, then the Holy Spirit has to guide the worshipper. We already established that knowledge, discernment, and holy wisdom as mentioned in the prayer for illumination are different from that of the world. In this context the worshipper prays to the Holy Spirit to guide in spiritual matters or things of heaven through the knowledge and wisdom, filled or received by the Holy Spirit.

The two modes of operation of the Holy Spirit in this guidance are through knowledge and wisdom. As this knowledge and wisdom are different and not of this world, it would be right to say that the Holy Spirit illumines us to know this knowledge and to be guided in this holy wisdom. The worshipper is filled by or receives the illumination of the Holy Spirit through the spiritual knowledge and wisdom. This thought can also be found in Basil for whom the Holy Spirit is the source of "illumination to every faculty in search of truth."[62] This has to be read along the lines of how the eastern fathers understand that the truth has to be searched for. However, as Basil puts it, truth has to be searched through the Holy Spirit. So

---

62. Basil, "On the Holy Spirit," 15.

The Prayer of Illumination

the human knowledge and wisdom that is operative in the search for the true understanding of the holy teachings is illumined by the Holy Spirit. After the illumination of the Holy Spirit it is the spiritual knowledge and wisdom that guides the human being in the search for the truth of the Gospel.

Furthermore, to be illumined means to be enlightened. When enlightenment occurs, a new thing is revealed. The process of revealing the new thing involves removal of the old or altering or modifying the old. The Bible also testifies to putting off the old self and putting on the new self. We can say that the old thing that is changed or modified involves sin and its consequences. Nevertheless, this process involves a change. It is a change from an existing state to a new state. We can say that when the worshipper is illumined the person is changed. Some form of purification or cleansing happens in this change. This becomes clear when we understand that St. Basil compares the Holy Spirit to the likeness of the sunbeam, whose kindly light falls on him who enjoys it as though it shine for him alone."[63] For Basil this illumination involves the first step of purification.[64]

A similar thought is found in Gregory of Nazianzus for whom purification has to happen for anyone to know anything of God.[65] To attempt to know God apart from this transformation represents the kind of knowledge, which according to Paul puffs one up with pride (1 Cor 8:1). For Gregory of Nazianzus, purification is a continual change and transformation is required to be able to know God. The Holy Spirit through illumination effects this purification. The human comes to a closer relationship with God when the Holy Spirit starts purifying the person through illumination. For Basil this purification is also the cleansing that happens in the person. As a result of this cleansing, the Spirit dwells in the person thereby making the person's soul spiritual. In this work of the Holy Spirit illuminating the worshipper, the knowledge of

---

63. Basil, "On the Holy Spirit," 15.
64. Basil, "On the Holy Spirit," 15.
65. Vinson, *Fathers of the Church*, 9.1–2; 15.1; 23.11; 32.12; 36.10.

The Prayer for Illumination: Address and Petition

the worshipper is "perfected by the presence of the Spirit."[66] We can say that the worshipper experiences purification or "cleansing through the illumination of the Holy Spirit." Since the Holy Spirit illumines through spiritual knowledge and wisdom, we can say that the mind, heart, soul, and spirit of the worshipper is purified. In other words the whole being of the worshipper is purified through the illumination of the Holy Spirit.

Illumination also has an understanding of being radiated by some form of light. It follows that something that was not clearly visible before is now more clearly visible. From the prayer for illumination we can say that the Spirit illumines the worshipper so that the worshipper can see the "truth." Basil writes that the Spirit shows forth the "truth in Himself, and, as Spirit of wisdom, in His own greatness revealing Christ the power of God and the wisdom of God."[67] Basil, in line with Matt 11:27, says that the Spirit reveals the Son because it is only through the Son can we know the Father. Further, Basil writes, "So souls wherein the Spirit dwells, illuminated by the Spirit, themselves become spiritual, and send forth their grace to others. Hence comes foreknowledge of the future, understanding of mysteries, apprehension of what is hidden, distribution of good gifts, the heavenly citizenship . . . abiding in God, the being made like to God, and highest of all, the being made God."[68] Notice that Basil is saying that through the illumination of the Holy Spirit, the person comes to know Christ, and through Christ, God the Father. Hence the illumination of the Holy Spirit leads to a revelation of the Triune God. Basil argues for such an illumination based on the words of Jesus.[69]

We can conclude that the MTL is eastern as it agrees with the eastern fathers that the illumination of the Holy Spirit is needed for the spiritual knowledge and wisdom to be revealed to the worshipper. The Holy Spirit illumines the worshipper through purification and cleansing from sin. As a result of this purification, the

---

66. Vinson, *Fathers of the Church*, 23.
67. Vinson, *Fathers of the Church*, 29.
68. Vinson, *Fathers of the Church*, 15–16.
69. John 16:14.

human knowledge, discernment, and holy wisdom is illumined. As a result of this illumination, a heavenly knowledge, discernment, and wisdom is available to the person through the Holy Spirit. The heavenly knowledge, discernment, and wisdom reveals a communion between the Father, the Son, and the Holy Spirit. Such a revelation of the Triune God is in line with the implicit address of the MTL to the Triune God. Through the illumination of the Spirit we see the light, i.e., God.[70]

Calvin draws a difference between a normal illumination and a "special illumination."[71] A normal illumination is that which happens when the human mind tries to understand something naturally. A "special illumination" is a "gift" from God.[72] This illumination, which is God's gift, happens due to God's "grace."[73] For Calvin, the work of illumination by the Holy Spirit in us results in evoking faith in us. For Calvin, without the light of the Holy Spirit "all is darkness."[74] The Holy Spirit regenerates the elect to see the light, i.e., the Heavenly Father.[75] This regeneration consists of the mind becoming "spiritually wise."[76] The mind thus becomes new, and becomes open to the "way to the kingdom of God" and the "spiritual mysteries." This regeneration evokes faith in the elect. Calvin, explaining John 1:12–13, says that through "faith [the Holy Spirit] leads [the elect] into the light of the gospel."[77]

We need to ask further: what exactly is the light of the gospel for Calvin? The Spirit illumines us, and as a result faith is evoked in us. Through this faith the Holy Spirit becomes our "inner teacher by whose effort the promise of salvation penetrates into our minds."[78] Calvin draws this conclusion from Eph 1:13; 2 Thess

---

70. Ps 36:9; John 1:9.
71. Calvin, *Institutes*, 2.2.18–19, 267–78.
72. Ps 36:9; John 3:27; 6:44; 1 Cor 12:3
73. Calvin, *Institutes*, 2.2.21, 281.
74. Calvin, *Institutes*, 2.2.21, 281.
75. Calvin, *Institutes*, 2.2.20, 278.
76. Calvin, *Institutes*, 2.2.20, 279.
77. Calvin, *Institutes*, 3.1.4, 541.
78. Calvin, *Institutes*, 3.1.4, 541. Also see Calvin, *Institutes*, 2.2.20, 279.

The Prayer for Illumination: Address and Petition

2:13; 1 John 3:25; 4:13; John 14:17. This penetration of the promise of salvation into our minds is the opening of the eyes of the mind for Calvin.[79] When the mind is opened in such a way, the mind becomes "capable of receiving the heavenly wisdom."[80] This is the work of illumination of the Holy Spirit that "unlocks for us treasures of the kingdom of heaven."[81]

We can conclude that for Calvin, the Holy Spirit illumines the mind of the elect by regenerating it. This regeneration results in the mind becoming new and spiritually wise. This evokes faith through the hearing of the Gospel, and it leads to a belief in Christ. Through Christ the elect become partakers in the salvation found in Christ and all the spiritual mysteries. This illumination is the regeneration that brings the elect "into the light of faith in his gospel."[82] This illumination helps the worshipper in understanding the truth of the holy Gospel. The MTL is not reformed in the sense that the theological analysis of the prayer for illumination does not suggest an illumination happening only in the elect. However, the MTL is reformed in the sense that the theological analysis of the prayer for illumination reveals some sort of regeneration happening in the worshipper. However, for Calvin the illumination of the Holy Spirit evokes faith in the elect. As a result of this faith the elect comes to a belief in Christ, and through Christ the elect is able to know and understand the mysteries of God.

---

79. Job 20:3.
80. Calvin, *Institutes*, 3.1.4, 542.
81. Rev 3:7.
82. Calvin, *Institutes*, 3.1.4, 542.

CHAPTER 3

The Prayer for Illumination
Fruit and Doxology

IN THIS CHAPTER WE'LL COVER the next two parts of the prayer for illumination, i.e., fruit and doxology.

Fruit

For purpose of analysis, I will divide the fruit section into two parts. The first half of the fruit section is as follows: *To be able to joyfully keep the commandments and to accomplish the Lord's will* (Syrian Liturgy); *to gladly obey the commands of God and to perfectly fulfill God's holy will* (MTL); *to honor God's name and instruct and edify God's Church* (Genevan Psalter).

We have to now dwell on the usages of "to be able to joyfully keep and to accomplish" (Syrian Liturgy); "to gladly obey and to perfectly fulfill" (MTL); and "to honor" (Genevan Psalter). In all three usages the issue under consideration is obedience to the will of God. All three usages also imply a possibility of not being able to *obey*. "To be able to keep" expresses the desire to keep the commandments, and at the same time points to the fear that the worshipper will not be able to keep the Lord's commandments.

The Prayer for Illumination: Fruit and Doxology

"To joyfully follow" conveys the desire to follow the commandments with joy. However, it also expresses the fear that there is an inherent possibility of following the Lord's commandments with regret or unhappiness. Similarly the usage "to honor" expresses the fear that there is a possibility of dishonoring God's name. It would mean that the obedience to the will of God can either be due to compulsion, a desire to obey, due to fear, or due to the existence of no other option for the person who is obeying. A preliminary analysis of the fruit specified in the prayer for illumination brings to the forefront the inherent *fear* on the part of the worshipper to *not* obey, or accomplish, or honor the will of God.

We can understand fear in three ways. First, the fear that comes out of respect, for example, between parent and child. In this scenario we fear out of love and intimacy toward the person. Second, the fear that comes when one is under an authoritarian rule. In this case we fear out of the perceived danger to our well-being. We could follow the commandments of God, or honor God's name out of the fear that if we do not do so God will do something bad to us. Third, the fear that comes out of compulsion to follow the laws of the world. We adhere to different laws of this world out of respect toward a common dignity of human life. Nevertheless, we adhere to the same laws more out of fear for the consequences of disobeying the law. It is a fear that comes out of compulsion to follow the law that governs us to obey the law in the first place. We would be following God out of a compulsion to obey the laws of God. Inherent in all these fears that lead to obedience is the human *will* or *desire* to obey.

"To be able to joyfully keep and to accomplish" (Syrian Liturgy), "to gladly obey and to perfectly fulfill" (MTL), and "to honor" (Genevan Psalter) would mean that the human *will* should either obey the will of God or should not obey the will of God. This obedience could be either out of fear or love. It also conveys that the best possible effort of human *will* and desire can either *be* able to obey or accomplish the will of God or it *will not be* able to accomplish the will of God. We can conclude that the fruit suggests that we, i.e., humans, have an important role to play in the perceived fruit, i.e., obeying or accomplishing the will of God, to come to reality.

If the prayer for illumination gives importance to the human *will* to be able to accomplish the will of God, it would mean that humans have an inherent capacity to follow the will of God. The illumination of the Holy Spirit enables the human *will* to obey the will of God, which would not have been possible without the illumination. The worshipper receives the help from the Holy Spirit through the illumination. After the illumination the worshipper is purified of sin. Before the purification the worshipper was bound to sin. Hence the worshipper was neither free nor able to follow the will of God. After the purification the human *will* is free on its own to grow in God.

Such an importance to the human effort or will is also found in the writings of St. Athanasius. For Athanasius the intelligence that resides in the soul can alone contemplate and perceive God.[1] The intelligence "distinguishes, recollects, and shews them [human] what is best."[2] Athanasius bases his argument upon Deut 30:14, wherein Moses teaches that the word of faith is within thy heart, and Luke 17:12, wherein Jesus says "the kingdom of God is within you." When all the sin that has stained the soul is gotten rid of, then the soul attains the "simplicity as it was made" so that humans "may be able by [intelligence that resides in the soul] behold the Word of the Father after Whose likeness [humans] were originally made."[3]

So the worshipper needs the illumination of the Holy Spirit to remove the stains of sin from the soul and to purify the soul. For Athanasius this illumination enables humans to be in a "state of virtue."[4] For Athanasius it is the state in which humans were originally made. Thus, Athanasius writes, "wherefore virtue hath need at our hands of willingness alone, since it is in us, and is formed from us. For when the soul hath its spiritual faculty in a natural

---

1. Athanasius, "Against the Heathen," in *St. Athanasius*, 2.30.3, 20.
2. Athanasius, "Against the Heathen," in *St. Athanasius*, 2.31.3, 20.
3. Athanasius, "Against the Heathen," in *St. Athanasius*, 2.34, 22.
4. Athanasius, "Against the Heathen," in *St. Athanasius*, 200.

The Prayer for Illumination: Fruit and Doxology

state virtue is formed. And it is in a natural state when it remains as it came into existence."[5] Humans are directed in their course according to their own free-will.[6]

We can conclude that the MTL is eastern in the sense that it agrees with the eastern fathers in stating that the enabling of the human *will* to obey the will of God is the fruit that is anticipated as a result of the illumination of the Holy Spirit. The eastern fathers go on to say that before the purification the worshipper was bound to sin. Hence, the worshippers *will* was not free. The worshipper was also not able to follow the will of God. After the purification the human *will* is free. Hence the worshipper's *will* is now free, and able to grow in God. However, theologically the MTL does not commit to the full freedom and ability of the human *will* to grow in God on its own. The worshipper hopes to gladly obey and to perfectly fulfill the will of God.

When we analyzed the anticipated fruit of the Genevan Psalter, i.e., "to honor God's name and instruct and edify God's Church," we came to a conclusion that also conveys a genuine fear of being unable to honor God's name. However, the usage of the word *honor* brings before us new possibilities. We use the term honor to denote privilege or high-esteem. In the prayer for illumination, the worshipper uses it in reference to God. The term honor also conveys that the one who is being honored, i.e., God, has some sort of claim over the one who is honoring, i.e., the worshipper. God has some sort of ownership over the worshipper. Hence the worshipper is *accountable* to honor God. It is for God that the worshipper honors God's name. Accountability means that the one who is being held accountable is also held responsible. Hence, the one who is being held accountable is bound to somebody else. The worshipper is responsible for faithfully honoring God's name. The worshipper is bound to the honor of God.

Similarly "to instruct and edify God's Church" is a fruit in which the worshipper is held accountable and responsible to bear

---

5. Athanasius, "Against the Heathen," in *St. Athanasius*, 200.

6. Athanasius, "Against the Heathen," in *St. Athanasius*; "The Festal Letters," XIX.7, 547.

fruit for the church of God. Since the fruit is borne for the church, the worshipper has an accountability and responsibility to God, and to God's church. The factor that controls the worshipper is something outside himself or herself, i.e., God, and the church. This would mean that the worshipper of his or her own will, and freedom cannot honor God's name or instruct and edify God's church. It is the illumination of the Holy Spirit that regenerates the elect. After this regeneration the Holy Spirit honors God's name, and instructs and edifies God's church through the worshipper.

This is made clear when we understand that for Calvin human nature is "faulty," "corrupted," and "vitiated."[7] For Calvin the "faculties of the soul are situated in the mind and the heart."[8] Calvin critiques the philosophers, the church fathers (sparing Augustine) who "extol the ability of the human will" to do good on its own.[9] Calvin is arguing against the human capacity to contribute in any small way to the grace of God and render it either effective or ineffective by free will. In other words, Calvin wants to completely negate the notion that humans by their free will can decide whether the grace received from God can be made to do good works or to do evil. Calvin wants to guard against the danger that humans by their *will* can either render the grace of God "ineffectual" or "confirm [the grace] by obediently following it."[10] Calvin drawing upon biblical sources (2 Cor 3:17; John 15:5) argues that without the help of God, or more exactly the enabling from the Holy Spirit, humans are not free and able to do the will of God.[11] So we can say that the Holy Spirit controls the worshipper's action.

We can conclude that in the Syrian Liturgy, the human agency is actively at work after the illumination. The Holy Spirit illumines the worshipper, and after the illumination the worshipper has the illumined will and freedom to obey the will of God. The human will and freedom cooperates with the operation of

7. Calvin, *Institutes*, 2.1.11, 254.
8. Calvin, *Institutes*, 2.2.2, 257.
9. Calvin, *Institutes*, 2.2.2–11, 257–69.
10. Calvin, *Institutes*, 2.2.6, 263.
11. Calvin, *Institutes*, 2.2.8, 265–66.

The Prayer for Illumination: Fruit and Doxology

the illumination of the Holy Spirit. The prayer for illumination in the Genevan Psalter anticipates the help of the Holy Spirit for the worshipper. An agency of the Holy Spirit is dominant and affective in the worshipper. However, after the illumination of the Holy Spirit, the human *will* and freedom is controlled by the Holy Spirit, because the human is now accountable, and responsible for the honor of God's name. The MTL is not eastern in the sense that it does not suggest the human agency is the one that cooperates with the operation of illumination of the Holy Spirit. The MTL is not reformed in the sense that it does not anticipates a full control of the human *will* and freedom by the Holy Spirit. However, the MTL suggests a middle ground of the eastern and reformed position. The MTL seems to suggest that there is a mutual cooperation of the agency of the Holy Spirit and the human agency. In this sense it is eastern and reformed.

The second half of the fruit section is as follows: *To be accounted worthy of the blessings and the mercies from the Lord* (Syrian Liturgy); *to be made worthy to receive the blessings and mercies of God* (MTL); *to bear the fruits of righteousness* (Genevan Psalter).

The usage of the verb "accounted" in the Syrian Liturgy conveys a different meaning than the verb "made" in the MTL. The verb *accounted* conveys an idea of something given beforehand, and the person to whom it is given being made accountable for what was given. This would mean that humans were already given the blessings and mercies of God. In this sense, one can think that the verb *accounted* has a different meaning than the verb *made*. However, it is good to note that it is in the fruit section of the prayer for illumination that the verb *accounted* is used. The worshipper is accountable to the blessings and mercies that flow because of the illumination of the Holy Spirit.

Such views can be found in Cyril of Jerusalem who opines that when the Holy Spirit illuminates the worshipper, the faith of the worshipper is raised "above man's power."[12] The illumination of the Holy Spirit operates in the worshipper. However, the impetus

---

12. Cyril, "Lecture V," in *St. Cyril of Jerusalem*, section 11, 31. For similar ideas see lectures 8.4, 48.

The Prayer of Illumination

is on the worshipper to cooperate with the Holy Spirit and to make the operation of the Holy Spirit effective. The worshipper will be accounted for this cooperation with the Holy Spirit. Gregory of Nazianzus also expresses similar views.[13]

However, the usage "to be made," as it appears in the MTL, conveys an act of continuous making, i.e., the process of being made worthy is an ongoing continual process by the Holy Spirit. It could mean that the worshipper is either not worthy or the worshipper is worthy, but not worthy enough to receive the blessings and mercies of God. In both cases a process of working through the worshipper is involved. The Holy Spirit works through the worshipper no matter what state the worshipper is in, either in a not worthy state or in a not worthy enough state, in such a way that the worshipper is made worthy. The Bible also testifies that the flesh is sinful, but amidst this sinfulness the Holy Spirit works through the human in such a way that the Holy Spirit rather than sin is at work.[14]

In the Genevan Psalter the prayer for illumination anticipates the worshipper "to bear fruits of righteousness." "To bear" means that something is produced as a result of a process happening inside the worshipper. If humans are to bear the fruits of righteousnesss, then the Holy Spirit has to work inside the human. Furthermore, one can understand "righteousness" as the act of doing something correct. However, the measuring rod for the act of doing the correct thing is not the right that the world deems to be right. Since this righteousness is a fruit of the illumination of the Holy Spirit, the measuring rod of this righteousness is the Holy Spirit. Since the measuring rod is the righteousness of the Holy Spirit, only the Holy Spirit can meet this requirement.

The Holy Spirit works in the worshipper in such a way that the Holy Spirit makes the worshipper bear the fruits of righteousness, which is in accordance to the will of God. This is clear when we understand that, for Calvin, God "illumines us with knowledge

---

13. Cyril, "Lecture V," in *St. Cyril of Jerusalem*, Oration 2.10–15, 207–8.
14. Rom 8:5–9; Gal 6:8.

The Prayer for Illumination: Fruit and Doxology

of himself" and "revives us from death."[15] Calvin goes on to argue, "who of us can boast that he has appealed to God by his own righteousness when our first capacity from well-doing flows from regeneration?"[16] Drawing upon biblical sources,[17] Calvin concludes that there is no righteousness in humans other than what God evokes in us through the Holy Spirit. Calvin, grounding his argument from 1 Cor 6:11, says that when the Holy Spirit illuminates us a cleansing happens. As a result of this cleansing, the blood of Jesus washes humans of their uncleanness. This cleansing produces a righteousness of God in us. Hence, we can say that the prayer for illumination anticipates that the fruit, i.e., to bear fruits of righteousness, are not borne by humans. Rather, the Holy Spirit implants in us this righteousness for us to bear it.

We can conclude that in the Syrian Liturgy the worshipper bears the fruit as a result of the illumination of the Holy Spirit. The worshipper is accounted worthy for bearing the fruit. However, the MTL acknowledges the limitation of the human *will* to worthily obey the will of God. As a result of this, the Holy Spirit works through the worshipper in such a way that the worshipper is made worthy day by day to receive the blessings and mercies of God. However, in the Genevan Psalter the prayer for illumination anticipates that the Holy Spirit is the active and only operating agent in making the worshipper bear fruits of righteousness. For Calvin when the Holy Spirit illumines the worshipper, regeneration happens in the worshipper. Following this regeneration the source of all acts of righteousness is the Holy Spirit.

Let us now analyze the doxology.

DOXOLOGY

Now and at all times (Syrian Liturgy); *Now and forever* (MTL).

---

15. Calvin, *Institutes*, 3.14.5, 771. Calvin draws this conclusion from John 5:25; Rom 4:17; 2 Cor 5:17; Eph 2:4–5.

16. Calvin, *Institutes*, 3.14.5, 772.

17. Isa 59:15–16; Hos 2:19, 23; 14:4; Rom 5:10; Col 1:21; 1 John 4:10; 1 Cor 6:11; 1 Pet 1:12; Phil 1:29.

The Prayer of Illumination

There is no mention of a doxology in the prayer for illumination in the Genevan Psalter. Here we are analyzing the doxologies of the Syrian and the Mar Thoma liturgies. The doxology of the Syrian and the Mar Thoma liturgies are similar in form. The doxology is predicated to the blessings and mercies that flow from God. As is evident, there is a reference to eternity in the usage "now and at all times" and "now and forever." Since it is predicated to God from whom all blessings and mercies flow, we can say the worshipper hopes that the nature of the illumination of the Holy Spirit and the resultant fruit will be "now and at all times."

The phrases "now and at all times" and "now and forever" cover the present time and the future time. "At all times" and "forever" also includes a third dimension of time other than present and future time. A past dimension is also included along with present and future. However, since the doxology is predicated to God and the blessings that flow from God, it would mean that the measuring rod for defining time is God. The Scriptures testify that God is eternal and everlasting. If God is eternal and everlasting then time would be included in God. Past, present, and future would be included in God. However, eternal means that there is no ending to God. If God does not have an ending then it follows that God does not have a beginning, for everything that begins has an ending. Hence, in God there is no beginning or end. God is eternal. Within this eternity of God, time is included, but God is more than time.

Such thoughts are also found in St. Athanasius who says that God is "Himself eternal . . . never beginning nor ceasing."[18] For Cyril the eternity of God means that God is not circumscribed in space.[19] Gregory of Nazianzus, claiming God to be eternal writes, "Eternity is neither time nor part of time; for it cannot be measured."[20] Gregory further writes, "God always was, and always is, and always will be; or rather, God always Is. For Was and Will

---

18. Athanasius, "On the Opinion of Dionysius," in *St. Athanasius*, 182.

19. Cyril, "Catechetical Lectures," in *St. Cyril of Jerusalem*, IV.5, VI.8, VIII.2, 20, 35, 48.

20. Nazianzen, "On the Theophany," in *St. Cyril of Jerusalem*, 347.

The Prayer for Illumination: Fruit and Doxology

Be are fragments of our time, and of changeable nature. But He is Eternal Being."[21]

We can conclude that the MTL is eastern in the sense that in the doxology of the prayer for illumination it alludes to the eternity of God. Time is included in God, but God cannot be limited by time. God has neither a beginning nor an end. God is eternal.

---

21. Nazianzen, "Second Oration on Easter," in *St. Cyril of Jerusalem*, 423.

Chapter 4

Conclusion

I STARTED THIS BOOK with the claim that in the Liturgy of the Mar Thoma Church we find a combination of eastern and reformed views of the Holy Spirit. Accordingly, I evaluated the doctrine of Holy Spirit as found in the prayer for illumination in the MTL in comparison with the teaching of eastern fathers and that of John Calvin. I will put together the conclusions according to the four sections of the prayer for illumination that I enumerated in the book, i.e., address, petition, fruit, and doxology. I will state where the MTL agrees or disagree with the eastern and the reformed point of view. I will also enumerate the implications for an eastern and reformed nature of the Mar Thoma theology.

ADDRESS

In the *address* of the prayer for illumination the MTL is eastern as well as reformed. It is eastern in the sense that the prayer is implicitly addressed to the Triune God. The explicit address to the Triune God in the prayer for illumination in the Genevan Psalter is similar to the implicit address to the Triune God in the prayer for illumination in the MTL. It is similar in the sense that

Conclusion: Fruit and Doxology

a communion in the Godhead is suggested by the address. Such a communion in the Godhead would suggest a Trinitarian implication to the theology of the MTC. It would mean that all the activity in the universe is controlled by a Trinitarian outlook. For example, to say that God creates would be to also say that the Son and the Holy Spirit also creates with God the Father. To pray to God would be to pray to the Triune God. To look forward to the second coming would be to look forward to the second coming of the Triune God. God would be understood as One who exists not in isolation; but, rather in communion within Godself. The Father, Son, and Holy Spirit exist as one in communion with each other.

PETITION

"To Fill," "To Receive," and "To Grant"

The analysis of the usages "to be filled," "to grant," and "to receive" helped us to understand that the MTL is eastern and reformed in suggesting a dependency on the Holy Spirit to live the Christian life. The MTL brings out the importance of the agency of the Holy Spirit to make the worshipper know God. The eastern theology advocates an indwelling presence of the Holy Spirit in the Christian. The reformed theology as advocated by Calvin advocates the Holy Spirit as a bond that unites Christ to the believer. The human nature is viewed as frail and in dire need of the filling of the Holy Spirit. Such a view of the human nature acknowledges the weakness of sin inherent in the human nature.

The Holy Spirit is sought to dwell in us to help us to grow spiritually in Jesus Christ. It is the grace of the Holy Spirit to dwell in this human nature even though it is frail. Such a continuous indwelling of the Holy Spirit suggests authority and the willingness of the Holy Spirit to work with humanity. The weakness of human nature cannot affect or stop the Holy Spirit to work with the human. The Holy Spirit is given for a purpose. The purpose is to maintain the communion with God. The active agent in the worshipper working toward the purpose of God is the Holy Spirit.

It also suggests that without the Holy Spirit, it is impossible to live the Christian life.

The usage "to grant" in the Syrian Liturgy suggests that the knowledge that is granted through the prayer for illumination governs the worshipper in understanding the divine words. A similar conclusion can also be drawn from the MTL. The MTL is eastern in this sense. A theological analysis of the Syrian Liturgy further reveals that the illumination elevates the capacity of the worshipper to make choices to accept the knowledge that is granted. Consequently, the worshipper starts cooperating with the knowledge that is granted. It is this cooperation of the worshipper that is the dominant agency after the illumination. The MTL is not eastern in that it does not suggest such a dominant agency of the worshipper.

However, the prayer for illumination of the MTL and the Genevan Psalter does recognize the human capacity to think, compare, and decide. The MTL is reformed in the sense that the prayer for illumination gives some consideration to the human capacity to know through its own natural faculties. However, this knowledge through the natural faculties reveals only a partial knowledge of God. A theological analysis of the prayer for illumination of the Genevan Psalter reveals that after the illumination the worshipper is controlled fully by the Holy Spirit.

The MTL is eastern and reformed in suggesting a dependency on the Holy Spirit to live the Christian life. A theological analysis of the MTL reveals that in suggesting the working after the illumination it leans both to the eastern and the reformed side. The MTL suggests a working of the Holy Spirit vis-a-vis with the cooperation of the worshipper. The worshipper is not controlled fully by the operation of illumination of the Holy Spirit. The cooperation of the worshipper is also not what controls the affectivity of the illumination of the Holy Spirit.

It suggests a mutual working or a co-agency of the Holy Spirit and the human. Inherent in human beings is the ability to do good. It is this ability to be good that motivates the human being to work along with the Holy Spirit. However, this ability to do good does not imply that the knowledge of humans about God is complete.

Conclusion: Fruit and Doxology

The working of the Holy Spirit is relational. For the world to be filled with the knowledge of God, human beings have to grasp this spiritual knowledge through the help of the Holy Spirit. The creation is dependent on the human beings for the knowledge of God to be actualized in actions. However, it would also mean that any deed on the part of human beings that would exploit the creation would convey a wrong knowledge of God. This calls for faithful and responsible stewardship on the part of the human beings. Human beings have to be faithful to the knowledge of God that would be imparted by the Holy Spirit, and to the good deeds that follow as a result of this impartation.

Knowledge of God

The prayer for illumination in the three liturgies sets the natural knowledge in contrast to the knowledge received through the Spirit. The MTL is eastern and reformed in this sense. The prayer for illumination of the Syrian, the MTL, and the Genevan Psalter points to the limitation of the human capacity to know God. The MTL is eastern and reformed in this sense.

However, the prayer for illumination in the MTL brings in the aspect of discernment, which includes a process of choice and decision on the part of the worshipper. The agency of the Holy Spirit is actively working with the agency of the human. As against this I argued that the usage of "to grant" in the Syrian Liturgy suggests that the worshipper after the illumination cooperates with the work of the Holy Spirit. However, the prayer for illumination of the MTL and the Genevan Psalter does recognize the human capacity to think, compare, and decide. The prayer gives some consideration to the human capacity to know through its own natural faculties. The MTL is reformed in this sense.

However, for Calvin this natural capacity of humans can lead to only a partial knowledge of God. The illumination of the Holy Spirit implants the true knowledge of God in the worshipper. Hence, theologically in the Genevan Psalter after the illumination of the Holy Spirit it is spiritual knowledge that is implanted in the worshipper and that is active in the worshipper. All three prayers acknowledge that knowledge of "divine words" has its source in the divine being, i.e., God. The prayer for illumination of the MTL is eastern and reformed in the sense that it acknowledges that knowledge of "divine words" has its source in the divine being, i.e., God. Hence, a spiritual discernment is needed. The worshipper prays to the Lord God to give such a knowledge or discernment. It brings out the excellence of the spiritual knowledge over that of the natural knowledge. Through the natural knowledge human beings can know God to some extent, but such knowledge is incomplete because it is incurred from the human faculty of intelligence. To grow in the excellent knowledge, i.e., spiritual knowledge, the Holy Spirit is required.

Divine Words

The MTL is eastern and reformed in that it agrees with the Syrian Liturgy and the Genevan Psalter on the theological position that Scripture reading implants a spiritual knowledge that is different from the knowledge of the world. The Gospel reading is important because of the life and events of Christ in it. The Bible as a book does not stand in itself as holy and authoritative. It is what the Holy Spirit does with the Bible that makes it holy and authoritative. God the Holy Spirit is asked to come on the scene, and make the Bible holy and authoritative through the illumination.

The words of the Gospel are sealed in the hearts of the hearers through the Holy Spirit. For a spiritual knowledge or discernment to be made possible, a prayer for illumination is needed. Thus, the illumination of the Holy Spirit happens in the "heart" during the reading of the Gospel. This is a reminder that we are not the lords of the Word, but rather God. Only God can speak God's Word. It is the Holy Spirit who communicates the words of the Bible in the way that God wants it to be communicated. This ensures that the divine inspiration by which the Bible was written is communicated to the worshipper.

Conclusion: Fruit and Doxology

The knowledge and discernment of [the] divine words, i.e., the words of the Gospel, are important for the life and sustenance of the church. The illumination of the Holy Spirit that happens in the heart of the worshipper ensures that the worshipper is connected to God through the Holy Spirit. If the worshipper is connected to God then it ensures that the church, which is constituted of individual members, is connected to God. In this connection a spiritual knowledge of God fills the church. This spiritual knowledge enables the members of the church to understand events associated with Christ and the Bible naturally as well as spiritually. Thus, the nature of the church as the body of Christ is intricately related to each and every member of the body.

After the hearing of the Gospel, the Holy Spirit enables the human to obey the commands of God. So the obedience to God is connected to hearing the Gospels. The Gospel contains the holy will of God, which the worshipper understands through the illumination of the Holy Spirit. The prayer for illumination enables the worshipper for the right reception of the will of God. The struggle is between the human will and God's will, human freedom and God's freedom. The worshipper has to obey the will of God as against his or her will. The hearing of the Gospel works through this struggle of human beings.

The hearing of the Gospel portion has to do with the words of Jesus or events associated with the life of Jesus. The prayer for illumination necessarily entails a Triune working in it. The worshipper prays to Lord God to send the Holy Spirit to know and discern the truth of the words and events associated with Jesus. The prayer for illumination of the MTL is Trinitarian in its way of working.

Holiness of the Gospel and Truth

For the eastern fathers, "truth" is something for which one searches. The MTL is eastern in the sense that a search for the truth is implied in its prayer for illumination. The worshipper perceives the different aspects of the holy Gospel and arrives at the goal of knowing *the* truth of the holy Gospel. The prayer for illumination of the MTL is not reformed in that it does not specify as to who will be "guided into the true understanding" of the holy Gospel. The Genevan Psalter has an underlying notion that only the elect will be "guided into the true understanding" of the holy Gospel.

However, the prayer for illumination of the MTL is reformed in that it also suggests a process of being "guided into the true understanding" of the holy Gospel. All three liturgies agree upon the need for the Holy Spirit to guide the worshipper in the truth of the holy Gospel. Such a help is sought so that the worshipper would know the truth or understanding of the holy Gospel. The Holy Spirit is the effective power that permeates the worshipper with the truth of the Gospel. It would follow that the authority of the Gospels and also the Scripture depends on the illumination of the Holy Spirit. It is the Holy Spirit who interprets the divine words to the worshipper. Hence, the worshipper would be able to understand and know the Spirit, and the true understanding in which the words were written because of the illumination of the Holy Spirit happening in the worshipper.

The holiness of the Gospel is dependent upon the illumination of the Holy Spirit. It is through the illumination that the worshipper understands and knows the divine inspiration in the Scriptures. Without the illumination of the Holy Spirit, the Scriptures stand as a normal book. Perhaps it will be revered because it is the Scripture of Christian religion. However, that does not guarantee that the worshipper will know the divine inspiration and knowledge filled in the words of the Scripture. In order to understand the true nature of the Scripture the Holy Spirit has to illumine the worshipper. It is worth giving a thought that if the knowledge and true understanding of the holy Gospel depends upon the illumination of the Holy Spirit, then what could stop the Holy Spirit to illumine others outside the worshipping community to discern the holiness and the knowledge filled in the Scripture?

Conclusion: Fruit and Doxology

Holy Wisdom

The worshipper petitions for the wisdom of God in order to understand the truth of the holy Gospel. Such a holy wisdom enlightens the worshipper. The prayer for illumination in the MTL is eastern and reformed as it maintains a distinction between worldly wisdom and godly wisdom. The prayer for illumination of the MTL leans more toward the reformed side as an explicit plea is made for the wisdom of God. In the Syrian Liturgy the worshipper prays for the gifts of God, which can include the wisdom of God among all the other gifts of God.

The MTL suggests that godly wisdom is beyond the understanding of the natural mind. Hence, the worshipper seeks the help of the Holy Spirit to fill the worshipper with the wisdom of God. It suggests that the realm of working of the illumination of the Holy Spirit is the mind. However, since the natural mind cannot fully grasp the knowledge of God in and of itself, the working of the illumination of the Holy Spirit should include other faculties of the human being. We could say that the illumination of the Holy Spirit works on the whole human being to fill him or her with the holy wisdom.

Illumination

The MTL is not reformed in the sense that the theological analysis of the prayer for illumination does not suggest an illumination happening only in the elect. However, the MTL is reformed in the sense that the theological analysis of the prayer for illumination reveals the communion of the Triune God. In the Genevan Psalter the illumination of the Holy Spirit evokes faith in the elect. As a result of this faith the elect comes to a belief in Christ, and through Christ the elect is able to know and understand the mysteries of God.

The MTL is eastern and reformed in the sense that it regards the Holy Spirit as the light that illumines us to know God. In the eastern fathers, illumination of the Holy Spirit involves purification. In Calvin, illumination of the Holy Spirit involves a regeneration of the elect. When we compare the explanation for purification in the eastern fathers with that of regeneration in Calvin, we come to a conclusion that both refer to one and the same thing. The MTL is eastern and reformed in the sense that theologically there is a similarity in the work of illumination of the Holy Spirit as understood by the eastern fathers and Calvin.

The MTL is eastern and reformed in the sense that theologically it views this purification or regeneration as happening in the whole being of the human. The MTL is not reformed in that it does not suggest it is only in the elect that the illumination happens. Calvin views the illumination to happen only in the elect. The eastern fathers emphasize more on knowing Christ and God the Father as the result of the work of illumination of the Holy Spirit. For Calvin, the Holy Spirit sheds light so that faith will develop in us through the hearing of the Gospel. Calvin stresses explicitly on the development of faith as the result of the illumination. This development leads the elect to the true knowledge of God. For the eastern fathers, the Holy Spirit sheds light so that we will be able to see the true light through the hearing of the Gospel. An explicit reference is not there to the development of faith through the hearing of the Gospel. Theologically, the MTC is eastern and reformed in that it suggests both the above possibilities happening in the worshipper. The worshipper is able to know Christ, and through Christ, God the Father. As a result of this Triune revelation, faith is evoked in the worshipper.

Eastern fathers argue that once the soul is purified, the intelligence that resides in the soul can understand the things of God in itself. However, Calvin maintains that the Holy Spirit is needed eternally to enable the human to contemplate and understand God, because any good that we do is of the Holy Spirit. Calvin wants to guard against the danger of extolling the human capacity to do good without any help of the Holy Spirit, resulting in holding the effectuality of the grace of God to depend on the will of humans to do good.

Conclusion: Fruit and Doxology

FRUIT

The MTL is not eastern in the sense that it does not suggest the human agency is the one that cooperates with the operation of illumination of the Holy Spirit. The MTL is not reformed in the sense that it does not anticipates a full control of the human *will* and freedom by the Holy Spirit. However, the MTL suggests a middle ground of the eastern and reformed position. The MTL seems to suggest that there is a mutual cooperation or a coagency of the Holy Spirit and the human. Thus, the MTL mediates the eastern and the reformed position in suggesting a coagency of the Holy Spirit and the human. In this sense it is eastern and reformed.

Thus, it acknowledges the struggle within human beings to follow the laws of God. However, the communion between the Holy Spirit and the human beings would mean that deep within ourselves there is something imprinted by God in our nature to seek God. This would also mean that the human nature is incomplete without the illumination of the Holy Spirit. The Holy Spirit is the One who completes the human nature as the Lord wants it to be. It follows that the human nature is elevated through the illumination of the Holy Spirit.

The prayer for illumination would suggest that the starting point of the work of the Holy Spirit is human heart. As a result of this internal work the effects are visible on the outside, i.e., through the actions. However, one should not lose sight of the Triune nature of the address of the prayer for illumination. It suggests that just as the Triune God is in communion eternally, the human beings have to be in communion with God and through God to the creation.

Thus, an ethical Christian life is associated with the Holy Spirit. The foundation of this ethical life is the Trinitarian communion. Such an ethics includes relationality, mutuality, humility, understanding the struggles of the creation, etc. The beginning point of such an ethics is the communion present in the Triune God. This communion does not exclude humanity or the creation. The very fact that the Holy Spirit works in a mutual relation with

The Prayer of Illumination

the human conveys a relational existence for the Triune God. This would mean that any exploitation of the creation is an act against the Triune God.

As against a general implication that is implied by "to fully obey" or "to be able to accomplish the will of God," the Genevan fruit, i.e., "to instruct and edify God's Church," is very specific. It could be said that the Holy Spirit illumines the worshipper toward the purpose of glorifying God and God's church. The Mar Thoma and the Syrian Liturgy suggests a glorifying of God and God's creation, not just the church.

As I concluded before, the MTL suggests a middle ground of the eastern and reformed position. The MTL seems to suggest that there is a mutual cooperation of the Holy Spirit agency and the human agency. This would mean that glorifying the creation requires faithful stewardship on the part of the worshipper. It would also mean that the Holy Spirit works through the illumination in the worshipper to bring about God's glory in the creation. This mutual relationality that exists with the Holy Spirit and the worshipper would extend to the creation.

The illumination also exposes the inadequacy of humans to live in communion with each other and the creation. We can understand human will and freedom as bound to sin. The illumination of the Holy Spirit sheds light on this human state. At the same time, the illumination empowers the human beings to be liberated from this bondage to sin. Thus, liberation from bondage depends on the continuous illumination of the Holy Spirit. The prayer for illumination is not only an invoking of the Holy Spirit in the liturgy, but it is also the important time of cleansing and purifying the human being.

I concluded that the Holy Spirit illumines the worshipper to understand the "inner meaning" of the Gospels, ie., Christ, and through Christ come to know God. The illumination of the Holy Spirit enables the worshipper to a life of relationality. Through illumination the worshipper comes to know the communion that exists in the Triune God. This illumination enables the worshipper to be in communion with the fellow brothers and sisters and

Conclusion: Fruit and Doxology

the creation. The mutual communion of the Holy Spirit with the worshipper enables the worshipper to live a life of humility. This humility comes from the fact that the Holy Spirit is continuously illumining the worshipper even though the worshipper does not deserve such a privilege. It is in living such a life that humans are most free, for we are fulfilling our human calling to love God and the creation.

DOXOLOGY

We can conclude that the MTL is eastern in the sense that in the doxology of the prayer for illumination it alludes to the eternity of God. Time is included in God, but God cannot be limited by time. God has neither a beginning nor an end. God is eternal.

I started off this book with the objective to theologically ground the eastern and reformed nature of the Mar Thoma Church. In the prayer for illumination, there are places where the MTL has similarities with the Syrian Liturgy and the Genevan Psalter. However, there are also dissimilarities as against the Syrian Liturgy and the Genevan Psalter. However, the uniqueness of the MTL is that at many places it puts forward a mediating position. The prayer for illumination suggests a middle ground that negotiates the two different positions of the Syrian Liturgy and the Genevan Psalter. Hence, I can arguably say that the MTL puts forward a mediating theology. This holds prospect to develop a mediating theology for the Mar Thoma Church.

Bibliography

Anaphora: The Divine Liturgy of Saint James The First Bishop of Jerusalem, According to the Rite of The Syrian Orthodox Church of Antioch. Published by Metropolitan Mar Athanasius Yeshue Samuel, 1967.
Athanasius. *St. Athanasius.* 4 vols. Edited by Philip Schaff and Henry Wace. A Select Library of the Nicene and Post-Nicene Fathers of the Christian Church 4. Second Series. Grand Rapids: Wm. B. Eerdmans, 1955.
Basil. *The Hexaemeron.* n.p.: Aeterna, 2016.
———. "On the Holy Spirit." In *St. Basil the Great on the Holy Spirit*, translated by David Anderson. Crestwood, NY: St. Vladmir's Seminary Press, 1980.
Bobrinskoy, Boris. *The Mystery of the Trinity: Trinitarian Experience and Vision in the Biblical and Patristic Tradition.* Crestwood, NY: St. Vladmir's Seminary Press, 1999.
Calvin, John. *Institutes of the Christian Religion.* 2 vols. Edited by John T. McNeill. Translated by Ford Lewis Battles. The Library of Christian Classics 20. Philadelphia: Westminster, 2006.
———. *Writings on Pastoral Piety.* Edited by Elsie Anne McKee. New York: Paulist, 2001.
Cyril. *St. Cyril of Jerusalem, St. Gregory Nazianzen.* Edited by Philip Schaff and Henry Wace. A Select Library of the Nicene and Post-Nicene Fathers of the Christian Church 7. Second Series. Grand Rapids: Wm. B. Eerdmans, 1955.
Dix, Gregory. *The Shape of the Liturgy.* New York: Continuum International, 1945.
Edwards, Denis. *Breath of Life: A Theology of the Creator Spirit.* New York: Orbis, 2004.
Elsie Anne Mckee, ed. *John Calvin: Writings on Pastoral Piety.* New York: Paulist, 2001.
John, Zachariah. "The Liturgy of the Mar Thoma Syrian Church of Malabar in Light of its History." Durham University, 1994. http://etheses.dur.ac.uk/5839/.
Malankara Mar Thoma Sabhayudae Kurbana Taksa. Tiruvalla: Mar Thoma, 2001.

Bibliography

The Mar Thoma Church: Order of Worship for Divine Service, Holy Qurbana, and Other Sacraments & Rites. New York: The Literature Society of the Diocese of North America and Europe, 2012.

Merriam-Webster Online Dictionary. "Knowledge." http://www.merriam-webster.com/dictionary/knowledge.

Missick, Stephen Andrew. "Mar Thoma: The Apostolic Foundation of the Assyrian Church and the Christians of St. Thomas in India." *Journal of Assyrian Academic Studies* 14 (2000) 52–59.

Nazianzen, Gregory. *St. Cyril of Jerusalem, St. Gregory Nazianzen.* Edited by Philip Schaff and Henry Wace. A Select Library of the Nicene and Post-Nicene fathers of the Christian Church 7. Second Series. Grand Rapids: Wm. B. Eerdmans, 1955.

Nyssa, Gregory. *Gregory of Nyssa: Dogmatic Treatises, etc.* Edited by Philip Schaff and Henry Wace. A Select Library of the Nicene and Post-Nicene Fathers of the Christian Church 5. Second Series. Grand Rapids: Wm. B. Eerdmans, 1955.

Old, Hughes Oliphant. *The Patristic Roots of Reformed Worship.* Zürich: Theologischer Verlag, 1975.

Špidlík, Tomáš. *The Spirituality of the Christian East: A Systematic Handbook.* Translated by Anthony P. Gythiel. Cistercian Studies Series 79. Michigan: Cistercian, 1986.

Thompson, Bard. *Liturgies of the Western Church.* Philadelphia: Fortress, 1961.

Varughese, Vazhayil Sakariah. "Religion, Renaissance and Protest: Sanskritization and Protestantization in Kerala, 1888–1936." PhD diss., Princeton Theological Seminary, 2003. http://search.proquest.com/docview/305313348?accountid=13316.

Vinson, Martha, trans. *The Fathers of the Church: St. Gregory Nazianzus: Select Orations.* Washington, DC: Catholic University of America, 2003.

Yousif, Patros. "East Syrian Spirituality—Basic Elements and Orientations." In *Oriental Churches Theological Dimensions,* 115–25, edited by Xavier Koodapuzha. Kottayam, IN: Oriental Institute of Religious Studies, 1988.

www.ingramcontent.com/pod-product-compliance
Lightning Source LLC
Chambersburg PA
CBHW070101100426
42743CB00012B/2630